Table of Content

Preface
Who is this book for?
Why I Wrote This Book
Internet
    DNS
        How DNS Works
        Benefits of DNS
    Hosting
    Types of Hosting
    HTTP
        How HTTP Transforms Your Missions
        Clear Requests, Understandable Data
            Actions, Not Just Words
            Secure and Reliable
        Key Takeaway
    Domain Names: Your Ship's Galactic Call Sign
        How Domain Names Guide Explorers
            Name, Not Numbers
                Organized Galaxy
                Claim Your Space
VS Code Editor
    Using VS Code to create a website
        Phase 1: Project Initialization
        Phase 2: Constructing the Webpage with Emmet
        Phase 3: Mission Launch
    HTML Syntax explained
        The Essential Tags
            Tags
            Attributes
        Common Code Components
            The Document Structure
HTML Forms
    How Forms and Validation Work
        Forms as Control Panels
        Validation is Your Safety Net

- Error Handling for Smooth Operations
  - Code Example: Transmission Console (Contact Form)
- Accessibility
  - How Accessibility Improves Your Crew
  - Key Practices
    - Labels and Structure
    - Beyond Sight
    - Testing: Make It Real
      - Evaluation Tools
      - Screen Readers (Test how your site sounds)
      - Color Accessibility
- Modern SEO
  - Behind the Scenes
    - Title Tags
    - Meta Descriptions A quick summary of what your webpage offers.
      - Metadata Example
        - Code Breakdown
        - What it Does
    - Semantic HTML: Use code in a way machines understand
      - Non-Semantic HTML example
        - The problem with this approach
      - Semantic HTML (Using meaningful tags)
        - What's better here
    - The Rise of the E-A-T (expertise, authoritativeness, and trustworthiness)
    - The UX Singularity
- CSS Basics
  - Example
    - CSS (Styling the status panel)
      - Explanation
        - Selectors
        - Properties and Values
  - CSS Flexbox
    - Flexbox Components
    - Flexbox Properties
    - justifyContent
    - Flexbox in Action
      - Explanation
        - The Container
        - The Items
        - display
        - flex-direction

- justify-content
- align-items
- Git: Your Code's Time Machine
  - How Git Saves the Day
    - Version History
    - Teamwork
    - Experiment Safely
  - Git Lingo
    - Repo
    - Commits
    - Branches
  - Installing Git on your machine
    - Verifying Installation
    - Git Commands
- Node.js: The JavaScript Engine
- npm: Your Ship's Parts Marketplace
  - The Synergy between Node and NPM
  - Installing Node and NPM on your machine
    - The NPM Package Manager
      - Command Line
    - Verification
    - How npm Streamlines Construction
      - No Reinventing the Wheel
      - Focus on Your Mission
      - Trusted Parts
    - Using npm
      - Find
      - Install a package
  - Common npm commands
  - Important Notes
    - package.json
      - This file is central to npm. It tracks project dependencies, scripts, etc.
    - Global Installs
- JavaScript
  - Running a JavaScript code with Node.js
  - JavaScript Variables
    - var
    - let: Flexible Crew
    - const: Your Specialists
  - Why This Matters
    - Organized Ship

- Fewer Mistakes
  - When to Use Which
- Variable Scope
  - Global Scope: The Starship's Public Address System
  - Local Scope: Mission Briefings in Specific Departments
  - Benefits of local variable:
    - Reduced Errors
    - Improved Code Readability
  - Maintaining Order on the Starship
- Global Scope
  - The Risks of Unguarded Communication: Global Variables
    - Namespace Collisions
    - Debugging Nightmares
  - Safer Alternatives
    - Targeted Communication
    - Secure Modules
    - Refactoring for Safety
      - Example
- Functions on the Bridge: Understanding Global Scope
  - Benefits of Global Functions
    - Reusable Tools
  - Potential Hazards
    - Name Clashes
    - Tight Coupling
  - Tips
    - Use Sparingly
    - Modules for Organization
  - JavaScript Naming Rules Your Starship's Code Navigation
    - Key Rules
      - Start Right
      - camelCase is King
      - Constructors Stand Tall
      - Off-Limits Words
    - Why Clear Naming Matters
      - Easy Reading
      - Smooth Maintenance
- JavaScript Prototypes: Your Starship's Crew Training Manual
  - The Academy (Prototype)
    - Blueprint for Success
      - Example
  - Building Your Crew

- Benefits of Prototypes
    - Efficient Training
    - Easy Updates
  - Advanced Concepts
    - Specialization
    - Inheritance
- JavaScript's Built-in Toolkit
  - Key Tools
    - Number
    - Math
    - Date
    - String
    - Function
    - Boolean
  - Why They Matter
    - Save Time
    - Clearer Code
- JavaScript Type Casting: Repurposing Your Resources
  - How It Works
    - Automatic Replicator
    - Tip
  - Why It Matters
    - Flexibility
    - Avoid Errors
  - Code example
- Data Structures
  - Arrays - Indexed Collections
    - JavaScript Arrays: Your Starship's Docking Bay
      - The Docking Bay Crew (Array Elements)
      - Accessing the Crew (Array Indexing)
      - Maintaining Order (Array Methods)
    - Benefits of an Organized Docking Bay
      - Data Grouping
      - Efficient Access
- Structure Data - JSON
  - The Rosetta Stone of Data
    - Communicating Across Alien Systems
    - Benefits of a Universal Protocol
      - Readability
      - Interoperability
      - Lightweight

- Decoding Transmissions and Sharing Data
- JavaScript Value Comparison Operators: Navigation and Targeting Systems
  - The programmer's Toolkit
    - Equality (== and ===)
    - Inequality (!=, <, >, <=, >=)
  - Conditional Logic
- Loop and Iterations
  - Break / continue - Maneuvering Through Your Code
    - break Evading Asteroids (Exiting Loops)
    - continue: Skipping Loop Iterations
      - Benefit: Code Optimization
- for…in statement Exploring Uncharted Systems
  - Scanning for Alien Artifacts
- while statement
  - Regulation
  - Reaching Your Destination
- do…while statement Loop
  - Engaging Emergency Warp
- The for loop
  - Following the Navigation Chart
  - Precise Maneuvers
- Conditional Statements
  - Switch
    - The Switch Expression
      - The default Case
  - If…else
    - Chaining for Complex Choices
- Throw statement
  - Red Alert
    - Example
  - Handling the Error
  - Why Use throw?
    - Prevention
    - Specific Errors
- Try, Catch, Finally
  - try…catch
  - Ensuring System Stability (finally)
  - Expressions and Operators
    - Assignment Operators
      - The Basics
    - Shorthand Operators: Efficiency Tools

- Addition Assignment (+=)
- Subtraction Assignment (-=)
- Multiplication Assignment (*=)
- Division Assignment (/=)
- Other Operators: Specialized Settings
- Key Points
- Comparison Operators
  - Equality and Inequality
    - Equal (==)
    - Strict Equal (===)
    - Not Equal (!=)
    - Strict Not Equal (!==)
  - Comparison Operators for Ordering
    - Greater Than (>)
    - Less Than (<)
    - Greater Than or Equal To (>=)
    - Less Than or Equal To (<=)
- Logical Operators
- Arithmetic operators
  - Basic Arithmetic
    - Addition (+)
    - Subtraction (-)
    - Multiplication (*)
    - Division (/)
  - Shorthand Assignment Operators
    - Increment (++)
    - Decrement (--)
  - Advanced Calculations
    - Modulus (%)
    - Exponentiation (**)
- String Operators
  - String Concatenation
  - String Access and Modification
    - Bracket Notation ([])
    - Methods like slice, substring, and substr
  - String Comparison
    - Comparison Operators (==, ===, !=, !==)
- Logical Operators in Control Flow
  - Logical operators AND and OR
    - Logical AND (&&)
    - Logical OR (||)

- Logical NOT (!)
- Comma Operators Evaluating Expressions Sequentially
- Side Effects and Common Uses
  - Scenario 1: Updating Multiple Variables Concisely
  - Scenario 2: Calling Functions for Sequencing
  - Warning: Potential Performance Implications
- Conditional operators
- Ternary Operator

Function
- Function Basics
- Function Parameters
  - Default Parameter Values
- Arrow Functions
  - Implicit Return
  - Lexical this
- Built in functions
  - Math Functions
  - String Functions
  - Array Functions
  - Control Flow Functions
- Benefits using Built in functions

Asynchronous JavaScript
- Non-Blocking Operations
- Promises and Callbacks
- Benefits of Asynchronous Operations
  - Improved Performance
  - Efficient Resource Management

setTimeout
- Delayed Execution
- Chaining setTimeout

setInterval
- Repeated Execution
- Continuous Monitoring

Promises
- Asynchronous Handling
- Promise States
- Benefits of Guaranteed Delivery
  - Error Handling
  - Chaining Operations

Async/Await
- Awaiting Results

- Benefits
  - Error Handling
  - Sequential Logic
- Callback
  - Passing a Function
  - A Symphony of Actions (Asynchronous Communication)
- Working with APIs
  - Making API Requests
  - A Wealth of Information at Your Fingertips (Data Retrieval)
  - Benefits of Universal Communication
    - Simplified Data Fetching
    - Promise-Based Handling
    - Versatility
- This Keyword
  - this in a function
    - Function Context
    - Function Calls
  - "this" in event handlers
    - Event Target
    - Event Delegation
    - Benefits of Responsive Controls
      - Event Delegation Efficiency
  - this in arrow functions
    - Lexical this
    - Lexical Inheritance
    - Benefits
      - Conciseness
      - Lexical Consistency
  - "this" in a method
    - Object Context
    - Method Calls
    - Benefits of Contextual Control
- Modules
  - Modular Construction (Import and Export)
- DOM Manipulation
  - Document Object Model
  - DOM Selection and Modification
    - getElementById
    - getElementsByClassName
    - querySelector
    - textContent

- innerHTML
- style
- Benefits
- Type Checkers - TypeScript
  - TypeScript vs JavaScript
    - JavaScript
    - TypeScript
  - Choosing the Right Crew for the Mission
    - Starting a new project
    - Maintaining a large codebase
  - TS Playground
    - What is the TS Playground?
    - Why use it
    - Start Playing!
  - Tsconfig.json
    - Customizing the Compiler
  - Typescript Types
    - The Perils of Loose Coupling (JavaScript and Unexpected Data)
    - Defining Data Types with TypeScript
  - Type Inference
    - Type Inference to the Rescue
  - Function Overloading
  - Namespaces
    - Conflicting Names and Access Modifiers
  - Classes
    - Building from Scratch (Traditional JavaScript Objects)
    - TypeScript Classes
    - Constructors, Inheritance, and Polymorphism
  - Tsc
    - What is TSC?
    - Why use it?
      - Automation
      - Type Safety
      - Integration
    - How to use it (simplified)
- Server Side Rendering - React
  - Vite
    - Traditional Development Workflow
      - Traditional workflow steps (simplified)
    - Vite to the Rescue
    - Development Server and Bundling for Production

- Creating a React Application With Vite
  - Prerequisites
  - Project Initialization
  - VS Code Integration
    - Project Structure
  - Running the Application
- React Components
  - Benefits of TSX
  - Components and Communication
    - Props (Incoming Data)
    - State (Internal Management)
  - When to Use Props vs State
- Conditional Rendering
  - JSX and Components
  - Conditional Statements - if/else
  - Ternary Operator
  - Logical Operators
- Rendering
  - Lists and Keys
    - React Lists
    - Avoiding Identity Crisis (The Importance of Keys)
    - Beam Up New Crew Members (Efficient Updates with Keys)
- Hooks
  - Traditional State Management
  - Introducing useReducer
- useMemo
  - Traditional Functions and Performance
  - Memoization with useMemo
  - useMemo and Component Updates
  - Basic hooks
    - useState
    - Components and State
    - Updating State
    - State and User Interaction
    - useEffect
      - Components and Side Effects
      - useEffect for Side Effects
      - useEffect for Data Subscriptions
      - Following Orders (useEffect Dependency Array)
- Routing - React Router
  - Components and Navigation

- Routing with React Router
  - In this example
  - Exploring the Holodeck (Dynamic Routing with Parameters)
- Styling
  - Traditional UI Development
  - React MUI
  - Customization and Theming
- Styled components
  - Traditional CSS and Challenges
  - Styled Components in Action
  - Styling Props and Dynamic Styles
- Testing
  - Why Testing is Important
  - Testing with Jest
  - Testing Different Scenarios
- API Calls
  - react-query
    - Challenges of Manual Data Fetching
    - Data Fetching with React Query
  - Forms
    - Traditional Form Handling
    - React Hook Form
    - Validation Made Easy
    - Benefits of React Hook Form
- State Management with Redux
  - Traditional State Management
  - Example of State management with Redux in a React application
  - Redux Toolkit
    - Traditional Redux
    - Redux Toolkit
    - Immutable Updates and Async Operations
    - Benefits of Redux Toolkit
- About the Author

Preface

Welcome to "Frontend Development 101 2024 with JavaScript, TypeScript, and React 18," a comprehensive guide to navigating the frontend web development landscape. In this book, we'll explore the fundamental concepts, best practices, and advanced techniques that define contemporary frontend development. As your guide, I, Rishi Gujadhur, am thrilled to lead you through this journey, whether you're a seasoned developer or a newcomer.

The table of contents outlines our expedition, from understanding the foundational elements of the internet to harnessing the power of cutting-edge tools and libraries like TypeScript and React 18. We'll delve into the mechanics of DNS, demystify the intricacies of HTTP, and explore hosting environments. From there, we'll navigate through the essentials of HTML, CSS, and JavaScript, laying a sturdy groundwork for our journey into more advanced topics. Throughout this odyssey, we'll encounter challenges, but armed with knowledge and the latest technologies, we'll navigate these obstacles with confidence and finesse. Whether it's mastering the art of DOM manipulation, harnessing the power of asynchronous JavaScript, or sculpting elegant user interfaces with React, we'll tackle each challenge head-on. In this ever-expanding universe of frontend development, adaptability and continuous learning are paramount. This book is a dynamic compass, guiding you through the currents of change and evolution in the realm of web development. With each chapter, you'll not only gain practical skills but also cultivate a mindset of curiosity and exploration. Whether you're charting a course for personal projects, professional endeavors, or intergalactic adventures, may this book serve as your trusty map, guiding you towards new horizons and boundless possibilities. Bon voyage, fellow explorer. Rishi Gujadhur

Who is this book for?

'Frontend Development 101 2024 with JavaScript, TypeScript, and React 18' is crafted with a diverse audience in mind, catering to both newcomers and seasoned professionals.

For Beginners: If you're new to web development, this book serves as an invaluable primer, providing a structured pathway for learning the foundational concepts and technologies. With clear explanations and practical examples, beginners can embark on their coding journey with confidence.

For Intermediate Developers: Intermediate developers will find this book to be an ideal resource for honing their skills and broadening their knowledge base. Dive into topics like asynchronous JavaScript, state management, API integration, etc.

For Experienced Professionals: Even seasoned professionals will discover valuable insights within these pages, as the book delves into advanced techniques, best practices, and emerging trends in frontend development.

Ultimately, 'Frontend Development 101 2024' is for anyone passionate about crafting immersive user experiences, building dynamic web applications, and pushing the boundaries of what's possible in the digital realm. Regardless of your background or experience level, if you possess a curiosity for learning, a drive for innovation, and a desire to create impactful digital experiences, then this book is for you. The adventure awaits.

Why I Wrote This Book

'Frontend Development 101 2024 with JavaScript, TypeScript, and React 18' is the culmination of my passion for frontend web development and my desire to empower others to embark on their own coding journeys. As the author, I've created this resource to demystify the complexities of modern frontend technologies and inspire readers to unlock their full potential as developers. Drawing from my own experiences in the field of web development, this book serves as a guiding light for those embarking on their journey into the world of web development. I aim to provide readers with a structured pathway for learning, equipping them with the knowledge, tools, and confidence necessary to succeed in the dynamic field of frontend development. Moreover, I've written this book with a deep sense of commitment to fostering inclusivity and diversity within the tech community. In an industry that is constantly evolving, it is essential to create spaces where individuals from all walks of life feel welcomed, supported, and empowered to pursue their passions. Through this book, I strive to cultivate a culture of inclusivity, where everyone feels inspired to contribute their unique perspectives and talents to the world of frontend development. Whether you're a curious beginner, a seasoned professional, or anyone in between, I invite you to join me on this journey of discovery, growth, and innovation.

Internet

DNS

How DNS Works

You try to access a website or communicate with a starship using its domain name. Your ship's computer contacts a DNS server, like consulting a galactic directory. The DNS server gets the domain name IP address. Your ship's computer establishes a connection using the IP address.

Benefits of DNS

Using DNS in your web application, communication and navigation become simpler. DNS translates complex alien addresses into user-friendly names, promoting seamless interaction between your website and any network encountered during interstellar voyages.

Hosting

Hosting, like a starbase, stores your web application and makes it accessible across the galaxy via the internet.

Types of Hosting

- Shared Hosting: Cost-effective sharing of resources suitable for smaller applications.

- Virtual Private Server (VPS) Dedicated space with more control and customization.

- Cloud Hosting: Scalable and flexible infrastructure ideal for varying traffic demands.

HTTP

How HTTP Transforms Your Missions

Clear Requests, Understandable Data

Send requests for lifeform analysis or enemy ship schematics – HTTP ensures the right data comes back in a format your crew can use.

Actions, Not Just Words

Need to update a planetary sensor network or report a distress signal? HTTP methods (GET, POST, PUT, DELETE) let you act, not just receive information.

Secure and Reliable

Encrypted communications (HTTPS) protect critical data, while error codes help you troubleshoot unexpected problems.

Key Takeaway

Integrating HTTP into your ship systems unlocks seamless communication with databases.

Domain Names: Your Ship's Galactic Call Sign

Forget navigating by complex IP addresses – that's like finding a star by its coordinates! Domain names make your web app discoverable and memorable throughout the cosmos.

How Domain Names Guide Explorers

Name, Not Numbers

A domain name like "[invalid URL removed]" or "Discovery-One.org" instantly tells other civilizations what you're about, replacing confusing IP addresses.

Organized Galaxy

Top-level domains (.com, .org, .mu, .shop.) act like star system sectors, hinting at your purpose (commerce, exploration...).

Claim Your Space

Registering your domain is like claiming a home star system. This ensures a unique identity and helps others find you.

VS Code Editor

First, access your web browser. Navigate to the official VS Code repository: https://code.visualstudio.com/download

There, download the appropriate installation package for your machine. Once the download is complete, initiate the installation sequence. Once the installation is complete, a gateway will open - the VS Code icon.

VS Code offers a plethora of features to augment your coding prowess. Explore the menus, brimming with options. Instruct the integrated terminal, a command prompt that obeys your spoken word (well, typed commands for now), to create new projects, folders, and files. The syntax highlighting, a multicolored aura, will illuminate your code, making it easier to decipher.

Using VS Code to create a website

Tools Required: VS Code: Your trusty code-ship. If not already aboard, refer to my previous transmission for installation instructions.

Phase 1: Project Initialization

Summon a Workspace: Within VS Code, designate a (folder) for your website.

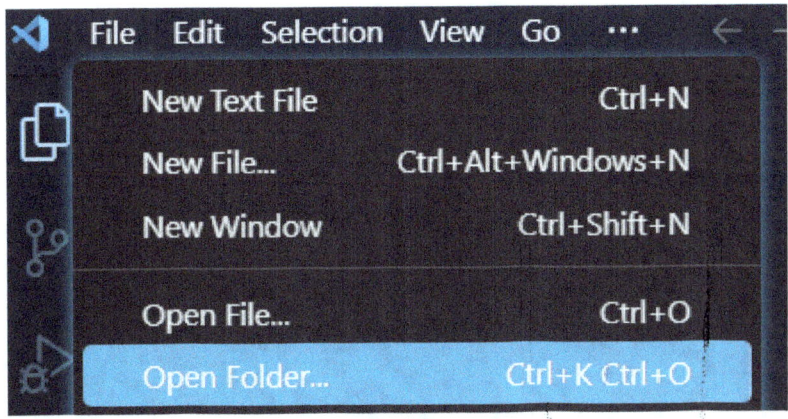

Manifest the HTML Blueprint: Within your workspace, create a new file and name it "index.html". This file serves as the structural foundation for your website.

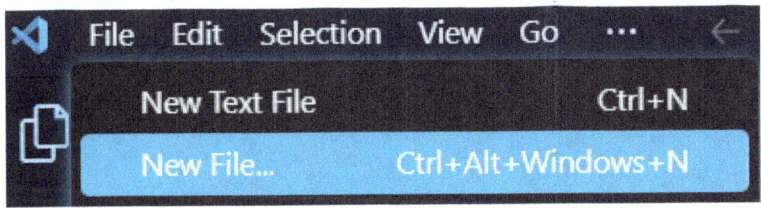

Phase 2: Constructing the Webpage with Emmet

The Skeletal Framework: Invoke the swift power of Emmet! Within your index.html file, type **! followed by the Tab key**.

A preformatted HTML skeleton will materialize before your eyes!

```html
<!DOCTYPE html>
<html lang="en">
<head>
    <meta charset="UTF-8">
    <meta name="viewport" content="width=device-width, initial-scale=1.0">
    <title>Document</title>
</head>
<body>

</body>
</html>
```

Phase 3: Mission Launch

Save your changes in VS Code and then summon your Web Browser: Locate your index.html within your workspace. With a right-click, choose "Open in browser". Your website will be projected into the vast digital expanse!

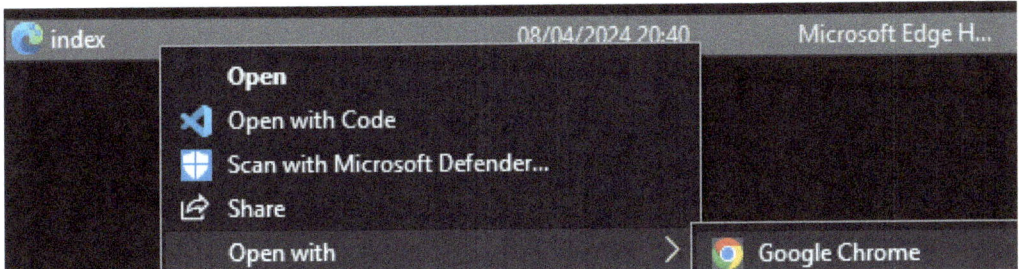

Preview of the webpage:

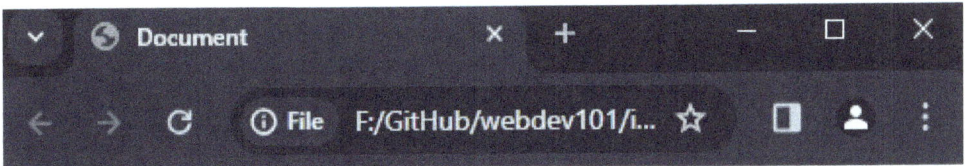

HTML Syntax explained

Let's delve into the fundamental building blocks of HTML, the code that shapes your website. Imagine HTML as a series of coded instructions, like transmissions to a powerful holographic projector, dictating the layout and content of your webpage.

The Essential Tags

Tags

Think of these as specialized beacons, bracketed with < and >. They mark the beginning and end of specific elements within your outpost. For instance, the <body> tag signifies the main content area, while <h1> creates a prominent heading.

Attributes

To further customize elements, employ attributes, additional details housed within the opening tag itself. For example, the src attribute within an <img> tag specifies the location of the image you wish to display.

Common Code Components

The Document Structure

Every HTML document begins with a <DOCTYPE> declaration, a sort of handshake with the web browser, establishing the document as HTML. Following this comes the <html> tag, the primary container for your entire web outpost. Nested within the <html> tag lie two crucial sections <head> and <body>:

<head>: This houses information not directly displayed on the page, like the page title (<title>) and links to external stylesheets (think blueprints for aesthetics).

<body>: This is the heart of your outpost, where all visible content resides - headings, paragraphs, images, and more!

- Headings (<h1> to <h6>): Establish a hierarchy of information with headings, sized from largest (<h1>) to smallest (<h6>).
- Paragraphs (<p>): These are the workhorses of your content, forming the bulk of your outpost's textual information.
- Images (<img>): Display visual components with the <img> tag, specifying the image source with the src attribute. Don't forget to include an alt attribute - a text description displayed if the image can't be loaded.

HTML Forms

Forget messy communication! HTML forms provide structured control panels for your crew to interact with ship systems and send clear messages across the galaxy.

How Forms and Validation Work

Forms as Control Panels

Forms organize input fields, buttons, and selections into intuitive panels. Crew members easily navigate them instead of deciphering cryptic command lines.

Validation is Your Safety Net

Imagine built-in sensors checking that warp coordinates are correct, energy levels are safe, and alien messages use the right format. That's validation protecting your starship, often supplemented with regex regular expressions.

Error Handling for Smooth Operations

Clear error messages (like "Invalid Coordinates") guide users to fix mistakes.

Code Example: Transmission Console (Contact Form)

Here's a basic example of a contact form resembling a starship's transmission console:

```html
<form>
  <div>
    <label for="name">Captain's Name:</label>
    <input type="text" id="name" name="name" required />
  </div>
  <div>
    <label for="message">Transmission Message:</label>
    <textarea id="message" name="message" required></textarea>
  </div>
  <button type="submit">Send Transmission</button>
</form>
```

This code snippet creates a simple form with a required name field and a message area.

The required attribute ensures these fields cannot be submitted empty.

Accessibility

Forget control panels only some of your crew can use! HTML accessibility ensures your ship's interfaces are designed for everyone, regardless of abilities.

How Accessibility Improves Your Crew

No Crew Member Left Behind: Screen reader support, keyboard navigation, and clear visuals mean every bridge officer can fully contribute.

Key Practices

Labels and Structure

HTML elements have meaning – use them correctly for screen readers and other assistive devices.

Beyond Sight

Allow keyboard-only use and design for various vision abilities.

Testing: Make It Real

- Use accessibility testing tools to find potential issues. Here are some popular accessibility tools.

Evaluation Tools

- WAVE (https://wave.webaim.org/) Browser extension for quick analysis.
- aXe by Deque (https://www.deque.com/axe/): Automated testing, detailed fixes.
- SiteImprove (https://siteimprove.com/en-us/accessibility/): Platform for deeper compliance.

Screen Readers (Test how your site sounds)

- NVDA (Windows, free): https://www.nvaccess.org/

Color Accessibility

- WebAIM Contrast Checker (https://webaim.org/resources/contrastchecker/)
- ColorBlindly (browser extension): Simulate color vision issues.

Modern SEO

The archaic keyword battles are over. Now, the Search Engine Overlords prioritize knowledge and user experience above all else.

Behind the Scenes

Title Tags

Your website name and specialties, clear in search results (e.g., "Starship Enterprise - Warp Repair")

Meta Descriptions A quick summary of what your webpage offers.

Metadata Example

```html
<head>
  <title>Starship Enterprise - Warp Repair, Medical Aid</title>
  <meta name="description" content="Our starship offers advanced warp drive repair capabilities and a fully-equipped medical bay for emergency assistance across the galaxy.">
  <h1>Welcome to the Starship Enterprise</h1>
  <h2>Warp Drive Specifications</h2>
  <p>Our warp core boasts a maximum sustainable speed of Warp Factor 9.5...</p>
</head>
```

Code Breakdown

- <head>: This section holds information about your page, not the content itself.
- <title>: Your ship's name! It shows in browser tabs and search results.
- <meta name="description">: A quick ad for your ship, shown in search results to attract attention.
- <h1>: The main heading of your page, like a chapter title.
- <h2>: Sub-headings for organizing information within your page.
- <p>: Basic paragraph text for the content people will read.

What it Does

- Helps search engines understand what your webpage is about.
- Makes your ship easier to find in search results with a clear title and description.

Semantic HTML: Use code in a way machines understand

Non-Semantic HTML example

The code below shows an example of non-semantic HTML code using generic div elements:

```html
1  <div id="header">
2    <div id="site-title">Starship Voyager</div>
3  </div>
4
5  <div id="main-content">
6    <div class="article">
7      <div class="article-header">Mission Log: Exploring the Delta Quadrant</div>
8      <div class="article-body">We've encountered a fascinating new species...</div>
9    </div>
10 </div>
11
12 <div id="footer">
13   <div>Copyright 2371 Starfleet</div>
14 </div>
```

The problem with this approach

No meaning: While humans might understand the purpose of these div elements based on their IDs and classes, search engines and assistive technologies don't get a clear picture of the content's structure.

Semantic HTML (Using meaningful tags)

```
1  <header>
2    <h1>Starship Voyager</h1>
3  </header>
4
5  <main>
6    <article>
7      <h2>Mission Log: Exploring the Delta Quadrant</h2>
8      <p>We've encountered a fascinating new species...</p>
9    </article>
10 </main>
11
12 <footer>
13   <p>Copyright 2371 Starfleet</p>
14 </footer>
```

What's better here

- header: Clearly labels the top section of your starship's webpage.
- main: Identifies the primary content area of your page.
- article: Defines a self-contained piece of content, like a mission log.
- footer: Designates the bottom section containing copyright info.

The Rise of the E-A-T (expertise, authoritativeness, and trustworthiness)

No longer anonymous entities, your authors shall be known. With schema markup, you'll transform their profiles into structured data beacons that Search Engines cannot ignore.

```html
<head>
    <title>Interstellar Sourdough: Baking Bread in the Void</title>
    <meta name="description" content="Join a seasoned galactic chef as they reveal the secrets to crafting the perfect sourdough loaf, even in the depths of space.">
    <meta name="author" content="Zara Quasar">
    <meta name="publisher" content="Cosmic Culinary Chronicles">
    <meta name="keywords" content="sourdough, interstellar baking, space bread, zero-g gastronomy">
    <meta name="robots" content="index, follow">
    <link rel="author" href="https://www.cosmiccuinarychronicles.galaxy/chef-zara">
</head>
```

In this example, the E-A-T elements are:

Expertise: The meta "author" tag identifies the author as "Zara Quasar", and the "link rel=author" points to a page that provides more information about the chef's expertise in interstellar baking.

Authoritativeness: The meta "publisher" tag identifies the website as "Cosmic Culinary Chronicles", which suggests the site has authority on the topic of space-based gastronomy.

Trustworthiness: The meta "description" tag provides a detailed, intriguing description of the content, which helps establish trust and relevance for the user. The "robots" tag indicates the page should be indexed and followed by search engines.

Your site must be a haven for weary travelers – blazingly fast on any viewport, its navigation as intuitive as a seasoned pilot's instincts. Responsive design is your key; wield frameworks like Bootstrap, TailwindCSS or MUI to bend the very code fabric to your will. Optimize your website's Core Web Vitals using tools like Lighthouse and PageSpeed Insights. Enhance performance by reducing render-blocking resources and employing techniques like lazy loading. Follow best practices such as code minification, browser caching, and CDNs for peak efficiency.

Video Transmissions from the Outer Rim

The search engines are not yet all-seeing – provide transcripts of your broadcasts. These text-based maps will illuminate your videos' content, transforming them into searchable star charts. Implement video and audio sitemaps to help search engines discover and index your multimedia content.

```html
<!-- Holo-Display Example -->
<holo-display width="800" height="600" controls>
  <source src="holo-video.mp4" type="video/mp4">
  Holographic projection unavailable.
</holo-display>

<!-- Sonic Transmission Example -->
<sonic-transmission controls>
  <source src="sonic-audio.mp3" type="audio/mpeg">
  Sonic playback not supported.
</sonic-transmission>
```

CSS Basics

Example

HTML (Structure of the status panel)

```html
<div class="status-panel">
  <h1>Warp Drive Status</h1>
  <p class="status-message">Warp Core: Offline</p>
  <button class="activate-button">Activate Warp Drive</button>
</div>
```

CSS (Styling the status panel)

```css
/* General panel styles */
.status-panel {
  padding: 20px;
}

/* Heading styles */
.status-panel h1 {
  text-align: center;
  margin-bottom: 10px;
}

/* Status message styles */
.status-message {
  font-weight: bold;
  color: orange; /* Warning color for offline status */
}

/* Button styles */
.activate-button {
  background-color: #007bff; /* Blue button */
  color: #fff;
  cursor: pointer;
}
```

Explanation

Selectors

CSS selectors target HTML elements by class names (status-panel, status-message, activate-button).

Properties and Values

- background-color, color: Control background and text colors.
- font-size, font-weight: Set text size and boldness.
- padding, margin: Add spacing for a cleaner layout.
- border, border-radius: Add a border and rounded corners.
- cursor: pointer: Make the button clickable.

CSS Flexbox

Imagine the Starship Enterprise bridge: The bridge is your web page, with UI elements as crew stations, control panels, and communication displays. Flexbox acts like the ship's internal gravity, organizing elements and adapting to different layouts.

Flexbox Components

Flex Container: The main section, akin to the USS Enterprise, provides structure to crew stations (child elements).

Flex Items: Individual stations arranged horizontally or vertically, flanking the captain's chair.

Flexbox Properties

flexDirection: Determines station arrangement, like tactical officer to the left and engineer to the right.

justifyContent

Aligns stations within the container, optimizing bridge operations.

alignItems: Controls vertical alignment for optimal visibility.

Flexbox in Action

Let's illustrate the starship status display example with some code:

```html
<div class="bridge-display"> <div class="status-station shields">Shields: 90%</div>
  <div class="status-station weapons">Phasers Ready</div>
  <div class="status-station navigation">Course Set</div>
</div>
```

```css
.bridge-display {
  display: flex;                      /* Activate Flexbox mode */
  flex-direction: row;                /* Crew stations arranged horizontally */
  justify-content: space-between;     /* Spread out the stations evenly */
  align-items: center;                /* Center stations vertically */

  width: 100%;                        /* Display takes up full bridge width */
  background-color: #333;             /* Futuristic dark background */
  padding: 15px;                      /* Some spacing around the stations */
}

.status-station {
  color: #00FFCC;                     /* Neon status text */
  border: 1px solid #00FFCC;          /* Neon borders */
  padding: 10px;
}
```

Explanation

The Container

The .bridge-display is our flex container. It establishes the rules for its crew stations (the status displays).

The Items

The .status-station divs are our flex items (shields, weapons, navigation).

display

flex makes the captain (container) use Flexbox for its crew.

flex-direction

row lines up the stations from left to right across the bridge.

justify-content

space-between spreads out the stations for optimal bridge visibility.

align-items

center ensures the crew stations remain centered vertically, even if one reports a longer status message.

Git: Your Code's Time Machine

How Git Saves the Day

Version History

Every change to your website's design is recorded, letting you undo mistakes or revisit old ideas.

Teamwork

Engineers work on updates without overwriting each other's work, even from different starbases.

Experiment Safely

Test new warp engines in "branches" without breaking the current setup.

Git Lingo

Repo

Your central blueprint archive.

Commits

Like saving different stages of your design.

Branches

"Parallel timelines" for new features.

Installing Git on your machine

Mission Objective: Establish Git, the sentinel of code history, upon your system.

The Installer: The primary approach is to secure the official Git installer. Launch your web browser and navigate to https://git-scm.com/downloads. Download the glistening installer file, compatible with your system's architecture.

Chocolatey - The Package Maestro: If you have Chocolatey already installed, a Windows package manager then the git installation is a mere command away! Open your terminal (Windows PowerShell or Command Prompt) and run:

- ```
  choco install git
  ```

Should you choose the Installer:

Launch the Installer: Locate the downloaded installer file and open it with a double-click. The installer shall present you with a series of options and settings, the defaults are typically suitable for a new installation. Word of Caution: During the Windows installation, you may be offered a choice of text editors. Select one with which you are comfortable, or explore a more powerful code editor option like Notepad++ or VS Code.

Verifying Installation

Summon your terminal of choice (Powershell or Command Prompt) and inquire Git's version via:

```
git --version
```

A response indicating the Git version confirms successful installation! You are now equipped with Git on your machine.
```

Git Commands

Basics	Branching	History and Rewinding	Remotes
git init: Initializes an empty Git repository in your current project folder. This is where you start tracking changes.	*git branch*: Lists all branches in your repo	*git log*: Displays the history of commits	*git clone <remote-url>*: Downloads a copy of an existing remote repository
git status: Shows the current state of your repository – what files are modified, staged for a commit, etc.	*git branch <branch-name>*: Creates a new branch	*git diff*: Shows changes between commits or between your working changes and the last commit.	*git remote add origin <remote-url>*: Adds a link to a remote repo under the name 'origin' (common convention)
git add <filename>: Stages a specific file to be included in the next commit. Use git add . to stage all modified files.	*git checkout <branch-name>*: Switches to a different branch.	*git reset <commit-hash>*: Resets your repo back to a specific point in history (use carefully).	*git push origin <branch-name>*: Uploads your local changes to the remote repo
git commit -m "Your commit message": Creates a snapshot of your current staged changes, with a descriptive message.	*git merge <branch-name>*: Merges the specified branch into your current branch (use with caution!).		*git pull origin <branch-name>*: Fetches updates from the remote repo and merges them into your local branch

Node.js: The JavaScript Engine

Think of Node.js as a powerful engine that allows you to run JavaScript code outside of a web browser. This opens up a whole new world of possibilities, from building web servers to creating command-line tools, all with the language you already know. In the next section we will be installing Node with the npm package supplier.

npm: Your Ship's Parts Marketplace

Forget building every part from scratch! npm is like a giant marketplace of pre-built spaceship components. Need a tool to connect to a database? Want a module to create fancy user interfaces? npm has got you covered.

The Synergy between Node and NPM

Node.js provides the power to run your JavaScript code, while npm lets you easily find and install the building blocks you need for your projects. Together, they form a dynamic duo that simplifies and accelerates web development.

Installing Node and NPM on your machine

The NPM Package Manager

To install programs, we'll utilize its built-in package manager. Different operating systems have their own package managers, so identify the one that governs your digital domain:

- For Ubuntu/Debian: One can use 'apt'.
- For Red Hat/CentOS: The yum package manager awaits your command.
- For Windows: We have multiple options!

Command Line

- Ubuntu/Debian: Open your terminal and run: sudo apt install nodejs npm
- Red Hat/CentOS: Open your terminal and run: sudo yum install nodejs npm
- Windows: A Choose-Your-Own-Adventure!

Option 1: The Official Installer: Launch your web browser and navigate to the official Node.js website. Download the installer compatible with your system's architecture. Once downloaded, double-click the installer and follow the on-screen instructions.

Option 2: Chocolatey - Open your terminal and run: `choco install nodejs`

Verification

Once the installation has completed, let's verify that Node.js and npm are operational. Open your terminal and type

```
node -v
```

This should display the installed Node.js version. To check npm, type

```
npm -v
```

A response indicating the version of both Node.js and npm confirms a successful installation!

How npm Streamlines Construction

No Reinventing the Wheel

Need a stellar navigation system? npm offers ready-made packages for common needs.

Focus on Your Mission

Spend less time on the basics, more time making your ship unique.

Trusted Parts

Many npm packages are community-tested, saving you debugging headaches.

Using npm

Find

Search the npm registry for the parts you need.

Install a package

A simple npm command to bring it on board:

Command	Description
npm init	Initializes a new Node.js project and creates a `package.json` file.
npm install <package-name>	Installs a package into your project and adds it to the dependencies in your `package.json` file.
npm uninstall <package-name>	Removes a package from your project and its dependencies.
npm update <package-name>	Updates a package to its latest version that's compatible with your project's requirements.
npm search <query>	Search the npm registry for packages matching your search terms.
npm publish	Publish your package to the npm registry, making it available to others.
npm start	Run the command specified in the "start" field of your `package.json`, often used to start a development server.
npm run <script-name>	Run a custom script defined in the "scripts" section of your `package.json`.

Common npm commands

Important Notes

package.json

This file is central to npm. It tracks project dependencies, scripts, etc.

Global Installs

Use the `-g` flag (e.g., `npm install -g create-react-app`) to install packages globally, making them available as command-line tools.

JavaScript

Running a JavaScript code with Node.js

Objective: Create a JavaScript file within VS Code and execute it using the power of Node.js.

- Initiate VS Code: Launch VS Code.
- Create a New Code-File: Enter the "File" command interface and select "New File". Or use a keyboard shortcut (Ctrl+N for Windows/Linux or Cmd+N on Mac).
- Name Your File: ensuring it ends with the .js designation, the mark of a JavaScript program. A simple "helloWorld.js" would suffice for this experiment.
- Inscribe Your Code: Within this newly created file, input your JavaScript code. For this demonstration, type: console.log("Hello World!");
- Preserve Your Work: Return to the "File" command interface and select "Save". Alternatively, use shortcut Ctrl+S (Windows/Linux) or Cmd+S (Mac). Save this file within a chosen directory.

Awaken the Node.js Engine:

Open VS Code's integrated terminal (View > Terminal or Ctrl+/ Cmd+ for the shortcut). Navigate to the directory where your code-file resides using the 'cd' command. Type node yourFileName.js (replacing 'yourFileName.js' with your script's filename) and press the enter key. Notice the output on the terminal: Hello World!.

Congratulations! You have harnessed the power of Node.js through VS Code! Now, expand your JavaScript knowledge with more JavaScript concepts and explore the boundless possibilities!

JavaScript Variables

var

The Old Way, **avoid** var is from an older era – its loose rules make your code unpredictable.

let: Flexible Crew

let is your go-to. Think of it as assigning crew to departments: they can only work their assigned shift.

```javascript
let helmOfficer = "Commander Spock"; // Only on duty in the bridge
```

const: Your Specialists

const is for values that never change – your captain, engine specs, etc.

```javascript
const maximumWarpSpeed = 9.9; // Constant, can't change
```

Why This Matters

Organized Ship

let and const make it clear who does what, making your code easier to understand.

Fewer Mistakes

const protects critical values, preventing accidental changes that could cripple your ship.

When to Use Which

let: For most variables that might change.

const: For values that must stay the same.

Variable Scope

Imagine your starship has different compartments and designated briefing areas. JavaScript's variable scope works similarly, defining where variables are accessible within your code.

Global Scope: The Starship's Public Address System

Variables declared outside of any function have global scope. They are accessible from anywhere in your program, like announcements broadcast over the ship's intercom system.

```javascript
let hullIntegrity = 100; // Globally accessible variable

function reportStatus() {
    console.log("Hull integrity at " + hullIntegrity + "%");
}

reportStatus(); // Can access hullIntegrity from within the function
```

Local Scope: Mission Briefings in Specific Departments

Variables declared within a function have local scope. They are only accessible within that function, like confidential information shared during departmental briefings.

```javascript
function activateWarpDrive() {
    let warpCoreTemperature = 70; // Locally scoped variable

    console.log("Engaging warp drive! Core temp at " + warpCoreTemperature + " degrees.");
}

// warpCoreTemperature is not accessible outside the function
```

Benefits of local variable:

Reduced Errors

Local scope prevents accidental modification of global variables, similar to how confidential briefings prevent unauthorized access to critical information.

Improved Code Readability

Local variables make code easier to understand by limiting their reach, similar to how focused departmental briefings provide clearer instructions.

Maintaining Order on the Starship

Use global variables sparingly, as they can lead to unintended side effects. Imagine overusing the intercom system creating confusion and information overload for the crew.

Local variables promote modularity and better organization, just like focused briefings in specific departments ensure crew members are well-prepared for their tasks.

Global Scope

The Risks of Unguarded Communication: Global Variables

In your starship's programming, global variables are like unguarded communication channels. While they allow any component to access data, they lead to these dangers:

Namespace Collisions

Two systems using the same variable name can cause unpredictable malfunctions. Imagine the warp core and impulse engines both using a variable called enginePower.

Debugging Nightmares

Global variables can be changed anywhere, making it frustrating to track down the root cause of bugs. Think of a garbled broadcast causing ship-wide confusion.

Safer Alternatives

Targeted Communication

Pass data as arguments to functions that need it, like sending specific orders to the right crew stations.

Secure Modules

Organize your code into modules with self-contained variables and functions. Imagine each system (warp core, impulse engines) having its own control panel.

Refactoring for Safety

Gradually replace global variables with function arguments or modules. It's about upgrading your code for clarity and reliability.

Example

```
1  // Old approach: reliance on global variable
2  let hullIntegrity = 100;
3
4  function reportDamage(damage) {
5      hullIntegrity -= damage;
6  }
7
8  // New approach: function argument for clearer control
9  function reportDamage(hullIntegrity, damage) {
10     return hullIntegrity - damage;
11 }
12
```

Functions on the Bridge: Understanding Global Scope

While global variables live *inside* functions, functions themselves can exist within the global scope. Think of these global functions as the master controls on your Web-app, accessible to anyone with clearance.

```
1  function activateWarpDrive() {
2    console.log("Warp drive engaged!");
3  }
4
5  function raiseShields() {
6    console.log("Shields raised!");
7  }
8  // Both functions are globally accessible
```

Benefits of Global Functions

Reusable Tools

They serve as universal tools for your starship crew, used anywhere onboard. Think of a displayMessage function for alerts.

Potential Hazards

Name Clashes

Just like duplicate system names, global functions with the same name can cause chaos.

Tight Coupling

Over-reliance on global functions can make your ship's systems harder to modify without breaking other things.

Tips

Use Sparingly

Global functions are best for truly universal tools. Most functions should be tucked into specific modules (like the weapons or engineering rooms).

Modules for Organization

Group related functions into modules to reduce name clashes. (Imagine a weapons module containing firePhasers and `launchTorpedoes.)

JavaScript Naming Rules Your Starship's Code Navigation

Think of JavaScript naming rules as the labeling system for your starship's controls. Clear and consistent naming makes your code easier to understand and maintain.

Key Rules

Start Right

Variable and function names must begin with a letter, underscore (_), or dollar sign ($). Examples: shieldLevel, _tempSensorReading, $commError.

camelCase is King

Use lowercase for the first word, then capitalize the first letter of each following word. Examples: activateWarpDrive, calculateHullDamage.

Constructors Stand Tall

Use PascalCase (all words capitalized) for constructor functions (blueprints for ship components). Example: PhaserArray.

Off-Limits Words

Avoid JavaScript keywords (words with special meanings like if, else, for). These are like protected commands on the ship's computer.

Why Clear Naming Matters

Easy Reading

Descriptive names make your code self-explanatory, like well-labeled ship controls.

Smooth Maintenance

You'll find it simpler to fix bugs or add features to your starship's systems when everything has a logical name.

```
let shieldStrength = 80; // Stores current shield level
function firePhasers() { ... } // Activates phaser weapons
```

JavaScript Prototypes: Your Starship's Crew Training Manual

Prototypes in JavaScript are like the Starship Academy – they provide the basic skills and knowledge for a specific type of object. Every object has a link to a prototype that gives it starting abilities.

The Academy (Prototype)

Blueprint for Success

A prototype object holds traits that all objects built from it will possess. Think of a standard class every crew member takes: navigation or communication.

Example

```javascript
const crewMemberPrototype = {
  species: "Human",
  rank: "Ensign",
  performDuty() {
    console.log("Crew member reporting for duty!");
  }
};
```

Building Your Crew

When you create new objects (crew members) from the prototype. They automatically inherit the prototype's properties and methods.

```javascript
const captainPicard = Object.create(crewMemberPrototype);
captainPicard.name = "Picard";
captainPicard.rank = "Captain";
```

Benefits of Prototypes

Efficient Training

Define standard skills once in the prototype – all "graduates" get them.

Easy Updates

Change the Academy's curriculum (prototype), and every crew member reflects the updates.

Advanced Concepts

Specialization

Constructor functions in prototypes let you further customize objects as they're created. (Think additional training for engineers and doctors)

Inheritance

Create new prototypes *based on* old ones for even more specialized crew roles.

JavaScript's Built-in Toolkit

Think of JavaScript's built-in objects as the standard-issue tools on your starship. They handle common tasks, letting you focus on your mission, not reinventing basic gear.

Key Tools

Number

Handles numbers for calculations (warp distances, fuel usage, etc.)

Math

Advanced calculations for engineering, like trigonometry for complex maneuvers.

Date

Track mission time, schedule crew shifts, and log important events.

String

Manipulate text for logs, displays, and analyzing incoming transmissions.

Function

Represents the core building blocks of your ship's software.

Boolean

True/false values for decision-making (shields up/down, system online/offline).

Why They Matter

Save Time

Avoid building common tools from scratch.

Clearer Code

Using standard tools makes your code easier to understand.

JavaScript Type Casting: Repurposing Your Resources

Sometimes on a long mission, you need to adapt existing materials for other uses. JavaScript's type casting lets you convert things like numbers, text, and true/false values into different forms to fit your program's needs.

How It Works

Automatic Replicator

Sometimes, JavaScript tries its best to convert values automatically. Adding a number and a text string that looks like a number ("5") will usually work.

Tip

For precise control, use Number(), String(), or Boolean() to force a specific conversion.

Why It Matters

Flexibility

Use data in ways it wasn't originally designed for. Think of turning temperature readings into display messages.

Avoid Errors

Clear casting can prevent unexpected results, like your replicator trying to make food out of engine parts!

Code example

```javascript
// Automatic conversion:
let result = 10 + "5"; // result will be the string "105"

// Explicit Conversion:
let sensorReading = "100";   // Originally a string
let temperature = Number(sensorReading); // Now a number for calculations

// User Input:
let input = prompt("Enter a number:"); // Input is always a string
let numericInput = Number(input);
```

Data Structures

Arrays - Indexed Collections

JavaScript Arrays: Your Starship's Docking Bay

Imagine your starship has a docking bay that can house multiple spacecraft. JavaScript arrays act like a virtual version of this docking bay, allowing you to store and manage collections of items in an ordered list. These items can be of various data types, making them a versatile tool for organizing information within your programs.

The Docking Bay Crew (Array Elements)

An array is a collection of values placed within square brackets []. Each value within the array is called an element, similar to individual ships docked in your bay. Elements can be of any data type: numbers, strings, booleans, or even other arrays (nested arrays).

```javascript
let dockedShips = ["Starship Enterprise", "Millennium Falcon", "Defiant"];
```

Accessing the Crew (Array Indexing)

You can access specific elements in an array using their index, which starts from 0. Imagine each docked ship having a designated spot in the bay. You can use the index within square brackets to target a specific ship.

```
console.log("Second ship in dock: " + dockedShips[1]);
// Accesses "Millennium Falcon"
```

Maintaining Order (Array Methods)

- Explore adding and removing elements from your array using methods like `push()`, `pop()`, and `shift()`.
- Practice using `sort()` and `reverse()` JavaScript provides various methods for manipulating arrays. Think of these as tools for managing the docking bay efficiently. You can add new ships (push()), remove ships (pop()), or sort them alphabetically (sort()).

```
1  dockedShips.push("Galactica"); // Add a new ship to the end
2  dockedShips.sort(); // Sort ships alphabetically
3
```

Benefits of an Organized Docking Bay

Data Grouping

Arrays allow you to group related information together, making your code more organized and easier to understand. Imagine having separate sections in your docking bay for different types of ships.

Efficient Access

You can quickly access specific elements within the array using their index, similar to how a well-organized docking bay allows for quick retrieval of specific spacecraft.

Structure Data - JSON

The Rosetta Stone of Data

JSON is a lightweight, text-based format for structuring data. Think of it as a simple interstellar language designed primarily for data exchange. It uses key-value pairs to represent data, making it human-readable and easily understandable for both humans and computers.

```
{
    "shipName": "USS Voyager",
    "captain": "Kathryn Janeway",
    "crewComplement": 150,
    "sensorRange": 10000, // Meters
    "warpCapable": true
}
```

Communicating Across Alien Systems

You can convert JavaScript objects into JSON strings and transmit them to other starships or alien civilizations. Imagine sending an encoded transmission that includes your ship's specifications or mission logs in a format that can be easily interpreted on the receiving end.

Conversely, you can receive JSON data (perhaps an alien distress signal or data from a space probe) and parse it into JavaScript objects to work with and understand the information within your program.

Benefits of a Universal Protocol

Readability

JSON's straightforward syntax makes it easy to understand and work with, even when exchanging data between vastly different technologies.

Interoperability

JSON is platform-agnostic, meaning it can be used across different programming languages and systems. Imagine communicating seamlessly with alien ships running their own unique software.

Lightweight

JSON's efficiency makes it ideal for transmitting data over communications channels, especially when bandwidth might be limited during deep space travel.

Decoding Transmissions and Sharing Data

- Learn how to use `JSON.stringify()` to convert JavaScript objects into JSON strings, ready for transmission.
- Practice using `JSON.parse()` to decode incoming JSON data (perhaps alien distress signals) into JavaScript objects that you can understand and work with.

JavaScript Value Comparison Operators: Navigation and Targeting Systems

Imagine navigating the vast expanse of space. Your starship relies on precise comparisons between sensor readings, target locations, and course corrections. JavaScript's value comparison operators act like the tools your navigation and targeting systems use to determine equality, difference, and other relationships between values.

The programmer's Toolkit

Equality (== and ===)

These operators check if two values are equal. The double equals (==) performs a loose comparison that may convert data types for comparison. Imagine the navigation officer roughly comparing two star positions to determine course correction.

The triple equals (===) performs a strict comparison that checks for both value and data type equality. Imagine the targeting system precisely comparing the enemy ship's location with your phaser banks' targeting data.

Inequality (!=, <, >, <=, >=)

These operators check relationships between values. The exclamation mark with equals (!=) checks for inequality. The less than (<), greater than (>), less than or equal to (<=), and greater than or equal to (>=) operators can compare numeric values.

```javascript
let enemyDistance = 1000; // Meters
let phaserRange = 800; // Meters

if (enemyDistance > phaserRange) {
    console.log("Warning: Enemy out of phaser range!");
} else {
    console.log("Fire phasers!");
}
```

Conditional Logic

These operators form the foundation of conditional statements (if/else) that allow your program to make decisions based on comparisons. Imagine the captain making strategic choices based on comparisons between enemy strength and your ship's capabilities.

Loop and Iterations

Break / continue - Maneuvering Through Your Code

Imagine navigating an asteroid field with your starship. You need precise control over your course to avoid collisions. JavaScript's `break` and `continue` statements act like navigational tools that allow you to control the flow of your program's execution, letting you jump out of loops or skip iterations when necessary.

`break` Evading Asteroids (Exiting Loops)

The `break` statement is used to terminate a loop (like `for` or `while`) prematurely.

```javascript
let hullStrength = 80;

for (let i = 0; i < 10; i++) { // Simulates damage over time
    hullStrength -= 10;

    if (hullStrength <= 50) {
        console.log("Warning: Critical hull damage!");
        break; // Exit the loop if hull integrity is too low
    }
}
```

`continue`: Skipping Loop Iterations

The `continue` statement skips the current iteration of a loop and jumps to the next one.

```javascript
let sectorsToExplore = ["Nebula", "Asteroid Field", "Uncharted Territory"];

for (let i = 0; i < sectorsToExplore.length; i++) {
    if (sectorsToExplore[i] === "Asteroid Field") {
        console.log("Skipping dangerous asteroid field!");
        continue; // Skip this iteration and move to the next sector
    }

    console.log("Exploring sector: " + sectorsToExplore[i]);
}
```

Benefit: Code Optimization

Using `continue` can sometimes improve efficiency by avoiding unnecessary calculations within a loop iteration.

for...in statement Exploring Uncharted Systems

Imagine venturing into a completely uncharted sector of space. You need a way to systematically scan and gather information from everything you encounter. The `for...in` loop acts like your starship's universal scanner, allowing you to iterate through the properties of objects, regardless of their origin or structure.

Scanning for Alien Artifacts

The `for...in` loop lets you loop through the enumerable properties of an object. Think of it as a universal scanner that can detect and report on various features of any alien structure or artifact you encounter during your exploration.

```javascript
let alienDevice = {
    energySignature: "Unknown",
    hullMaterial: "Adamantium",
    functionality: "Unidentified"
};

for (let property in alienDevice) {
    console.log("Detected property: " + property + ", Value: " + alienDevice[property]);
}
```

while statement

Imagine your starship needs to travel vast distances at warp speed. The `while` loop acts like your ship's warp core regulator, continuously checking a condition and executing a block of code as long as that condition remains true. This allows for sustained actions as long as the specific criteria are met.

Regulation

The `while` loop has two parts: a condition and a code block. The code block executes repeatedly as long as the condition evaluates to `true`. Think of it as the warp core constantly monitoring a specific parameter (like reaching a desired warp factor) and maintaining that level as long as the condition is true (warp core stable, sufficient dilithium reserves).

```javascript
let warpCoreStable = true;
let warpFactor = 1;

while (warpCoreStable && warpFactor < 9) { // Loop continues as long as both conditions are true
    warpFactor++;
    console.log("Engaging warp drive! Warp factor: " + warpFactor);

    // Simulate random warp core instability
    if (Math.random() > 0.5) {
        warpCoreStable = false;
    }
}

console.log("Warp drive disengaged.");
```

Reaching Your Destination

The loop eventually terminates when the condition becomes `false`. The `while` loop is ideal for situations where you need to perform an action repeatedly until a certain condition is met.

do...while statement Loop

Imagine encountering a critical situation during your interstellar voyage, like a sudden attack from a hostile alien fleet. You need to initiate an emergency warp jump immediately. The `do...while` loop acts like your ship's emergency warp drive activation system, ensuring a crucial action happens at least once, even if the condition for sustained travel might not be immediately true.

Engaging Emergency Warp

The `do...while` loop is similar to a `while` loop, but with a key difference. The code block executes at least once, then the condition is checked on line 9 as shown below:

```javascript
let warpCoreReady = false; // Simulates initial instability

do {
    console.log("Initiating emergency warp jump!");
    // Simulate warp core stabilizing during the jump sequence
    warpCoreReady = true;

    // Additional actions during the jump (like initiating evasive maneuvers)
} while (!warpCoreReady); // Loop repeats as long as the core is unstable

console.log("Warp jump successful!");
```

The for loop

Imagine navigating your starship on a meticulously planned course through a vast and unexplored nebula. The `for` loop acts like your ship's autopilot, allowing you to execute a set of instructions a specific number of times, following a clear plan to reach your destination.

Following the Navigation Chart

The `for` loop has three parts separated by semicolons: initialization, condition, and increment/decrement. It provides a structured way to iterate over a specific number of steps.

```javascript
for (let i = 0; i < 5; i++) { // i is the loop counter
    console.log("Taking sensor readings at sector " + (i + 1));
    // Perform actions or calculations at each iteration
}
```

Precise Maneuvers

The initialization statement sets up a loop counter variable (often `i`). The condition checks if the counter has reached the stopping point. The increment/decrement statement updates the counter after each iteration.

Conditional Statements

Switch

Imagine your starship encounters various alien species during its travels. Each species has established diplomatic protocols. The `switch` statement acts like your ship's protocol officer, efficiently identifying the encountered alien race and activating the corresponding communication protocol.

The Switch Expression

The `switch` statement evaluates an expression (often a variable holding the alien race identifier). Think of the protocol officer scanning a signal from the approaching vessel to determine its origin.

```javascript
switch (alienRace) {
    case "Zolarians":
        console.log("Initiate Zolarian greeting protocol.");
        break;
    case "Klingons":
        console.log("Raise shields and open a communication channel.");
        break;
    default:
        console.log("Maintain neutral stance and identify alien race.");
}
```

The `default` Case

The `default` case is an optional catch-all that executes if none of the `case` values match the switch expression. Imagine encountering an unknown alien race. The protocol officer would initiate a default procedure to identify them peacefully.

If...else

The `if...else` statement is the foundation of conditional logic in JavaScript. It checks a condition and executes a block of code if the condition is `true`. Optionally, an `else` block can provide alternative code if the condition is `false`. Think of the captain issuing orders based on incoming sensor data. If enemy ships are detected (condition true), the captain might order battle stations to be manned (code block for battle mode). Otherwise (else block), the ship might maintain its current course.

```javascript
let enemyDetected = true; // Sensor data

if (enemyDetected) {
    console.log("Red Alert! Prepare for battle!");
} else {
    console.log("Maintain course and speed.");
}
```

Chaining for Complex Choices

You can chain multiple `else if` statements together to create more intricate decision trees. Each `else if` checks a new condition only if all previous conditions were `false`. Imagine the captain having a hierarchy of responses based on the threat level. If a large enemy fleet is detected (condition 1), the captain might order full battle readiness. If only a small scout ship is found (condition 2), the captain might order increased vigilance.

```javascript
let enemyShipClass = "Battlecruiser";

if (enemyShipClass === "Battlecruiser") {
    console.log("Prepare for full battle engagement!");
} else if (enemyShipClass === "Scout") {
    console.log("Increase sensors and defense protocols.");
} else {
    console.log("Maintain course and continue observation.");
}
```

Throw statement

In JavaScript, the `throw` statement lets you trigger your own custom errors, acting like a signal for problems within your code.

Red Alert

The `throw` statement is like your ship's emergency alert. It forcefully creates an exception (error) when something unexpected happens.

Example

If your warp core is damaged, you might `throw new Error("Warp core breach imminent!")`.

Handling the Error

A `try...catch` block acts like your emergency response protocol:

- The `try` block contains code that might cause problems.
- The `catch` block activates if a `throw` statement is triggered within the `try` block, handling the error.

Why Use `throw`?

Prevention

Stop your program before a small issue becomes a catastrophic failure.

Specific Errors

Create custom error objects to provide more detailed information about the problem.

Try, Catch, Finally

This trio of statements is used to identify, isolate, and resolve critical issues.

try...catch

The try...catch block is the foundation of error handling. The try block encapsulates code that might potentially throw an error (like a malfunctioning warp core). The catch block defines how to handle the error if it occurs. Think of your engineer isolating a malfunctioning warp core section (try block) and then implementing repairs or initiating backups (catch block) if an error (warp core malfunction) arises.

```
try {
    // Code that might malfunction (e.g., warp core overheating)
    engageWarpDrive();
} catch (error) {
    console.log("Warp core overheating! Initiating emergency shutdown.");
    // Implement repairs or switch to auxiliary warp core (error handling)
}
```

Ensuring System Stability (finally)

The finally block (optional within a try...catch block) executes code regardless of whether an error is thrown or not, and even if the try block exits prematurely.

```
try {
    engageWarpDrive();
} catch (error) {
    console.log("Warp core overheating! Initiating emergency shutdown.");
    // Implement repairs or switch to auxiliary warp core (error handling)
} finally {
    console.log("Warp core status logged for further analysis.");
    // Always reset core temperature controls
}
```

Expressions and Operators

Assignment Operators

Assignment operators are essential tools for directly changing values within your program.

The Basics

= The fundamental assignment operator. It sets a variable to a specific value

Example: let enginePower = 50;

Shorthand Operators: Efficiency Tools

Addition Assignment (+=)

Adds a value to a variable and assigns the result back to the same variable. Think of the engineer using a tool to gradually increase engine power (enginePower += 10).

Subtraction Assignment (-=)

Subtracts a value from a variable and assigns the result back. Imagine using a tool to decrease shield strength (shieldStrength -= 5).

Multiplication Assignment (*=)

Multiplies a variable by a value and assigns the result back. Imagine adjusting phaser beam intensity (phaserIntensity *= 1.5).

Division Assignment (/=)

Divides a variable by a value and assigns the result back. Imagine calculating remaining fuel based on travel time (fuelRemaining /= travelTime).

```
1  enginePower += 10;  // Increases enginePower by 10
   (equivalent to enginePower = enginePower + 10)
2  shieldStrength -= 5;   // Decreases shieldStrength
   by 5
```

Other Operators: Specialized Settings

- %= Gives you the remainder of a division (useful for inventory checks).
- **= Calculates exponents for things like power drain over time.

Key Points

- Use = to copy values between variables.
- Shorthand operators are perfect for frequent number tweaks.

Comparison Operators

Comparison operators act like your ship's verification protocols, allowing you to compare values and make critical decisions during your voyage.

Equality and Inequality

Equal (==)

Checks if two values are equal, regardless of data type (can be misleading at times). Imagine comparing a string course code ("Alpha Centauri") to a variable accidentally assigned the same value as a number.

Strict Equal (===)

Compares both the value and data type, ensuring a true match. Imagine the pilot needing to confirm the course code matches not only the value but also that it's a string.

Not Equal (!=)

Checks if two values are not equal. Imagine checking if the current sector is not hostile territory.

Strict Not Equal (!==)

Similar to != but performs a strict comparison.

```
1  let courseCode = "Alpha Centauri";
2  let target = "Alpha Centauri"; // String
3  let sector = "GN-12"
4
5  console.log(courseCode == target); // Outputs: true (even though target
   is a number)
6  console.log(courseCode === target); // Outputs: true (strict comparison)
7  console.log(courseCode != sector); // Outputs: true
8
```

Comparison Operators for Ordering

Other comparison operators help determine if a value is greater than, less than, or falls within a certain range.

Greater Than (>)

It checks if the value on the left is greater than the value on the right. Imagine targeting only ships closer than 5000 kilometers (`distance < 5000`).

Less Than (<)

It checks if the value on the left is less than the value on the right. Imagine prioritizing shields if hull integrity is less than 20% (`hullIntegrity < 20`).

Greater Than or Equal To (>=)

It checks if the value on the left is greater than or equal to the value on the right. Imagine needing to initiate repairs if shields are at or below 50% (`shieldStrength >= 0.5`).

Less Than or Equal To (<=)

Checks if the value on the left is less than or equal to the value on the right.

Logical Operators

JavaScript offers logical operators (&& - AND, || - OR, ! - NOT) that combine comparison operators to create more complex conditions. Imagine needing to avoid asteroids that are both larger than 50 meters and within 1000 meters of the ship.

```javascript
let asteroidSize = 75;
let asteroidDistance = 800;

if (asteroidSize > 50 && asteroidDistance < 1000) {
    console.log("Warning! Evasive maneuvers required!");
}
```

Arithmetic operators

Arithmetic operators act like your engineers' toolset, allowing them to perform essential mathematical operations on numerical data critical.

Basic Arithmetic

Addition (+)

It adds two values together. Think of the engineer calculating the total power output by combining warp core and impulse engine contributions (`totalPower =warpCoreOutput + impulseEngineOutput`).

Subtraction (-)

It subtracts one value from another. Imagine calculating remaining fuel by subtracting fuel used from the initial amount (`fuelRemaining = initialFuel - fuelUsed`).

Multiplication (*)

It multiplies two values together. Imagine calculating the impact force of a phaser blast by multiplying weapon power by distance (`impactForce = phaserPower * distance`).

Division (/)

It divides one value by another. Imagine calculating average engine efficiency by dividing total power output by fuel consumption (`efficiency = totalPower / fuelUsed`).

```javascript
let warpCoreOutput = 1200;
let impulseEngineOutput = 300;
let initialFuel = 800;
let fuelUsed = 150;
let phaserPower = 100;
let distance = 200;

console.log("Total power output:", warpCoreOutput + impulseEngineOutput); // Outputs: "Total power output: 1500"
console.log("Fuel remaining:", initialFuel - fuelUsed); // Outputs: "Fuel remaining: 650"
console.log("Phaser impact force:", phaserPower * distance); // Outputs: "Phaser impact force: 20000"
```

Shorthand Assignment Operators

Increment (++)

It increments a variable by 1. Think of the engineer quickly raising a shield power setting (`shieldPower++`).

Decrement (--)

It decreases a variable by 1. Imagine rapidly lowering phaser power (`phaserPower--`) during a close encounter.

Advanced Calculations

JavaScript provides additional arithmetic operators for specific calculations:

Modulus (`%`)

It calculates the remainder of a division operation. Imagine calculating remaining torpedoes after a volley (`torpedoesRemaining %= 6`).

Exponentiation (`**`)

It raises a number to a power. Imagine simulating power drain over time (`energyReserves **= 0.95`).

String Operators

String operators act like your communication tools, allowing you to manipulate and combine text data for effective messaging.

String Concatenation

The plus sign (+) acts as a string concatenation operator, combining two or more strings into a single string. Think of the captain using the universal translator to combine a species' greeting ("chirp chirp") with a request for landing clearance ("landing request").

```javascript
let greeting = "Greetings, ";
let speciesName = "Zarquon";
let message = greeting + speciesName;

console.log(message); // Outputs: "Greetings, Zarquon"
```

String Access and Modification

JavaScript provides methods for accessing and modifying individual characters within a string

Bracket Notation (`[ ]`)

Used to access a specific character at a particular index (position) within the string. Imagine the communications officer carefully selecting specific characters within a message to ensure accuracy.

```javascript
let message = "Warp drive engaged.";
console.log(message[0]); // Outputs: "W"
(accessing the first character at index 0)
```

Methods like `slice`, `substring`, and `substr`

These methods extract substrings from a string based on specified starting and ending positions (or lengths). Imagine the captain editing a message by removing an outdated status report using `slice`.

String Comparison

Like comparison operators for numbers, JavaScript allows string comparisons.

Comparison Operators (==, ===, !=, !==)

These operators compare strings based on their character order.

```javascript
let sectorDesignation = "GN-12";
let targetSector = "GN-12";

console.log(sectorDesignation === targetSector); // Outputs: true (strict comparison)

```

String Search Methods

JavaScript offers methods like `indexOf` and `lastIndexOf` to search for substrings within a string and return their position (index). Imagine the science officer using these methods to search for specific keywords within an intercepted alien transmission.

```javascript
let transmission = "Warning: Incoming fighter squadron detected.";
let keywordIndex = transmission.indexOf("fighter squadron");

if (keywordIndex !== -1) { // Checks if keyword was found (not -1)
    console.log("Warning! Enemy fighters detected!");
}
```

Logical Operators in Control Flow

Imagine following a set of instructions based on whether a specific alien species is hostile or friendly. In this comprehensive section, we'll explore various aspects of logical operators and control flow in programming. We'll begin by introducing Logical AND (&&) and Logical OR (||), followed by a discussion on navigating through an Asteroid Field with Logical NOT (!). We'll then enhance our multitasking abilities with Comma Operators and fine-tune starship performance by understanding Side Effects and Common Uses. Through practical scenarios, such as updating multiple variables concisely and sequencing function calls, we'll grasp the potential performance implications and learn efficient Warp Core Maintenance techniques using Comma Operators. Additionally, we'll explore conditional operators, including the Ternary Operator for quick decisions. By mastering these concepts, programmers can write concise, expressive code and conduct efficient evaluations, crucial skills for navigating the vast expanse of programming challenges.

Logical operators AND and OR

JavaScript provides logical operators that combine Boolean expressions (true or false statements) to create more intricate decision-making logic.

Logical AND (&&)

Returns true only if both conditions on either side of the operator are true. Imagine the pilot needing to activate shields only if the enemy ship is both firing weapons (condition 1) and within firing range (condition 2).

```javascript
let enemyFiringWeapons = true;
let enemyInRange = true;

if (enemyFiringWeapons && enemyInRange) {
    console.log("Shields activated!");
}
```

Logical OR (||)

Returns true if at least one condition on either side of the operator is true. Imagine the captain needing to take evasive maneuvers if the forward shields are failing (condition 1) or the aft shields are depleted (condition 2).

```javascript
let forwardShieldsFailing = true;
let aftShieldsDepleted = false;

if (forwardShieldsFailing || aftShieldsDepleted) {
    console.log("Evasive maneuvers initiated!");
}
```

Logical NOT (!)

Inverts the logical state of a condition. Imagine needing to perform an action only if the current course is not safe (which means the safe course condition must be negated using NOT).

```javascript
let isSafeCourse = false;

if (!isSafeCourse) {
    console.log("Warning! Course correction required!");
}
```

```javascript
let warpCoreCritical = true;
let lifeSupportFailing = true;

if (warpCoreCritical && lifeSupportFailing) {
    console.log("Emergency protocols initiated!");
}
```

Comma Operators Evaluating Expressions Sequentially

The comma operator (,) in JavaScript acts primarily as an expression separator. It evaluates each expression it separates from left to right, but ultimately returns only the value of the **last** expression. Imagine your engineer performing multiple routine maintenance tasks, like checking a pressure gauge (expression 1) and then refilling coolant (expression 2). The comma operator ensures both tasks are completed, but only the coolant refill level (result of the second expression) is considered for further actions.

```javascript
let warpCoreTemperature = checkWarpCoreTemp(); // Expression 1
let coolantLevel = refillCoolant(5); // Expression 2

console.log("Coolant level at", coolantLevel, "% after refilling."); // Outputs only coolant level (last expression)
```

Side Effects and Common Uses

The comma operator's true power lies in its ability to trigger **side effects**. Side effects are actions that happen during expression evaluation, such as modifying variables, calling functions with side effects (like printing to the console), or performing actions that alter the program state. The comma operator allows you to chain expressions together, even if the results of the earlier expressions aren't directly used.

Scenario 1: Updating Multiple Variables Concisely

Imagine the engineer needing to adjust warp core temperature (expression 1) and monitor pressure levels (expression 2) during a maneuver. The comma operator allows both adjustments to occur within a single line.

```
warpCoreTemperature -= 10, checkPressureLevels();
// Adjust temp & check pressure (side effect)
```

Scenario 2: Calling Functions for Sequencing

Imagine needing to display a warning message (function call with a side effect) only after performing a critical calibration (another function call). The comma operator ensures the calibration happens first, followed by the message display.

```
calibrateWarpCore(), displayWarning("Calibration complete!");
```

Warning: Potential Performance Implications

While comma operators can be handy for specific situations, overuse can make code less readable. It's generally recommended to prioritize code clarity over extreme conciseness achieved through excessive comma operator use.

Conditional operators

Ternary Operator

The ternary operator (sometimes called the conditional operator) provides a concise way to express a simple if-else statement in a single line.

```javascript
let enemyShipDetected = true;
let action = enemyShipDetected ? "Raise shields!"
  : "Maintain course.";
console.log(action); // Outputs: "Raise shields!"

let hullStrength = 70;
let hullStatus = hullStrength > 50 ? "Operational"
  : "Warning: hull breach detected!";
console.log(hullStatus); // Outputs: "Warning: hull breach detected!"
```

```javascript
let enemyShipDetected = true;
let shieldsOnline = false;

if (enemyShipDetected && !shieldsOnline) {
    console.log("Red Alert! Evasive maneuvers!");
} else {
    console.log("Maintain course and prepare phasers.");
}
```

Function

Function Basics

Functions in JavaScript are reusable blocks of code that perform specific tasks. Think of a tricorder, a versatile tool used for scans and readings. A function named `scanSensorData` could process sensor readings from various parts of the ship.

```javascript
function scanSensorData(sensorType) {
    // Code to process sensor data based on sensorType
}

scanSensorData("warpCore"); // Specifying sensor type during function call
```

Function Parameters

Default parameters act like pre-set settings on your engineering tools.

Default Parameter Values

JavaScript functions can have default parameter values assigned to their arguments. These defaults are used when the argument is omitted during the function call. Default parameters provide flexibility by allowing you to override the default value when needed.

```javascript
function scanSensorData(sensorType = "engine") { // "engine" is the default parameter
    console.log("Scanning", sensorType, "sensor data.");
}

scanSensorData(); // Uses the default parameter ("engine")
scanSensorData("warpCore"); // Overrides the default with "warpCore"
```

Arrow Functions

Arrow functions act like your ship's efficient crew members, providing quick solutions to problems without the bulk of traditional function declarations.

```javascript
// Traditional function
function activateShields() {
    console.log("Shields raised!");
}

// Arrow function (same functionality)
const activateShields = () => {
    console.log("Shields raised!");
}
```

Implicit Return

For functions with a single expression in their body, arrow functions provide an implicit return statement, making the code even more concise. Imagine your crew instantly reacting to situations without needing to explicitly state a return value.

```javascript
// Traditional function
function getShieldStrength() {
    return 75;
}

// Arrow function (implicit return)
const getShieldStrength = () => 75;
```

Lexical this

Arrow functions inherit the "this" context from their surrounding code, unlike traditional functions which have their own "this" context. Imagine your crew members seamlessly working within the current system or ship section, inheriting the context of their location.

```javascript
let officerName = "Lt. Commander Spock";

const announcePowerLevels = () => {
    console.log("Current power levels at " + this.officerName + "'s station: 90%");
};

announcePowerLevels(); // Outputs: "Current power levels at Lt. Commander Spock's station: 90%"
```

Built in functions

Here are some common categories of built-in functions in JavaScript:

Math Functions

Perform mathematical calculations, essential for navigation, targeting, and resource management. (e.g., `Math.sqrt()` for square root, `Math.random()` for generating random numbers)

String Functions

Manipulate text data, crucial for communication protocols, ship logs, and displaying information. (e.g., `.toUpperCase()` to convert to uppercase, `.slice()` to extract substrings)

Array Functions

Work with arrays of data, used for storing sensor readings, crew manifests, and mission objectives. (e.g., `.push()` to add elements, `.join()` to combine elements into a string)

Control Flow Functions

Control the flow of your program, allowing for decision-making and repetitive tasks. (e.g., `if...else` for conditional statements, `for` loops for iterating)

```javascript
// Example using built-in functions:
let courseCorrectionAngle = Math.atan2(10, 20); // Calculating angle for course correction
let destinationName = "Alpha Centauri B";
let message = "Greetings from starship Enterprise. We are approaching " + destinationName.toUpperCase() + "."; // Using string functions for communication

```

```javascript
// Example using built-in functions for different purposes:
let phaserFrequency = parseFloat("23.4 kHz"); // Parsing sensor data (string to number)
let shieldsOnline = true;
if (shieldsOnline) {
    console.log("Diverting power to phaser banks for attack.");
} else {
    console.log("Shields down! Evasive maneuvers initiated!");
} // Using control flow for decision-making

```

Benefits using Built in functions

- Reduced code duplication: Built-in functions eliminate repetitive coding.
- Improved readability: Clear function names enhance understanding.
- Consistent functionality: Built-in functions ensure reliability across browsers and environments.

Asynchronous JavaScript

Asynchronous programming in JavaScript acts like your ship's efficient multitasking system, allowing it to handle multiple operations without getting bogged down.

Non-Blocking Operations

Traditional JavaScript code execution is synchronous, meaning the program waits for one task to finish before moving on to the next. Asynchronous programming breaks this mold. Think of your starship performing essential tasks like scanning for nearby star systems (asynchronous operation) while simultaneously plotting its course on the main computer (synchronous task).

```javascript
// Synchronous example (waits for scan to complete before continuing)
let starSystemData = scanForNearbySystems();
console.log("Plotting course based on star systems: " + starSystemData);

// Asynchronous example (continues plotting course while scan runs)
scanForNearbySystems()
    .then(data => console.log("Plotting course based on star systems: " + data));
console.log("Continuing with other ship operations...");
```

Promises and Callbacks

Asynchronous operations often involve waiting for external data or actions, like sending messages to a distant outpost or waiting for a sensor scan to complete. JavaScript provides mechanisms like promises and callbacks to handle these situations. Imagine sending a message to a friendly space station (asynchronous operation) and receiving a response (data) later through a callback or promise resolution.

```javascript
// Using callbacks
requestSuppliesFromStarbase( (supplies) => {
    console.log("Received supplies from starbase: " + supplies);
});

// Using promises
requestSuppliesFromStarbase()
    .then(supplies => console.log("Received supplies from starbase: " + supplies));
```

Benefits of Asynchronous Operations

Improved Performance

By not blocking the main thread, asynchronous programming allows your program to feel more responsive and avoid stalling while waiting for external data. Imagine your ship's computer continuing to function smoothly even while waiting for a response from a distant outpost.

Efficient Resource Management

Asynchronous operations prevent the program from tying up resources waiting for slow tasks. Think of your ship being able to perform other essential functions while waiting for a sensor scan, optimizing its processing power.

setTimeout

The `setTimeout` function acts like your ship's internal chronometer, allowing you to schedule events to occur at designated points in time.

Delayed Execution

The `setTimeout` function takes two arguments: the code to be executed (a function) and the delay time in milliseconds. Think of the pilot setting a timer on the chronometer (delay time) to initiate a specific course correction maneuver (code to be executed).

```javascript
let courseCorrectionAngle = 15; // Degrees

setTimeout(() => {
    console.log("Initiating course correction by " +
courseCorrectionAngle + " degrees.");
}, 3000); // Execute the function after 3 seconds (3000 milliseconds)

console.log("Continuing with current course...");
```

Chaining `setTimeout`

You can chain multiple `setTimeout` calls to create a sequence of events happening at different intervals. Imagine the pilot using the chronometer to trigger a course correction (first `setTimeout`), followed by activating the shields (second `setTimeout`) after a brief delay.

```javascript
setTimeout(() => {
    console.log("Activating shields!");
}, 1000); // After 1 second

setTimeout(() => {
    console.log("Initiating course correction by 20 degrees.");
}, 2000); // After 2 seconds

```

setInterval

The `setInterval` function acts like your ship's engineer, performing tasks at consistent intervals, keeping your vessel running smoothly.

Repeated Execution

The `setInterval` function takes two arguments: the code to be executed (a function) and the interval time in milliseconds. Think of the engineer setting up an automated system (the function) to continuously monitor critical systems (every `interval` time).

```javascript
let engineTemperature = 70; // Celsius

const monitorEngineTemperature = () => {
    console.log("Engine temperature stable at " + engineTemperature + " degrees Celsius.");
};

setInterval(monitorEngineTemperature, 2000); // Monitor every 2 seconds (2000 milliseconds)
```

Continuous Monitoring

`setInterval` is ideal for simulating ongoing processes or repeatedly checking for changes. Imagine the engineer initiating continuous scans (the function) for nearby space anomalies (every `interval` time)

```javascript
const scanForSpaceAnomalies = () => {
    console.log("Scanning for space anomalies...");
    // Simulate anomaly detection here
};

setInterval(scanForSpaceAnomalies, 5000); // Scan every 5 seconds (5000 milliseconds)

```

Promises

Promises act like your ship's communication officers, ensuring reliable exchange of information and handling the results of these tasks efficiently.

Asynchronous Handling

Promises provide a mechanism for handling asynchronous operations. Think of your communication officer adeptly handling multiple incoming messages (asynchronous tasks) without blocking critical ship operations.

```javascript
// Synchronous approach (waits for scan to complete before continuing)
let starSystemData = scanForHabitablePlanets();
console.log("Plotting course to nearest habitable planet: " + starSystemData);

// Asynchronous approach using Promises
scanForHabitablePlanets()
    .then(data => console.log("Plotting course to nearest habitable planet: " + data));
    console.log("Continuing with other ship operations...");
// No waiting!
```

Promise States

A Promise can be in three states: pending (waiting for completion), resolved (operation successful with data), or rejected (operation failed with an error). Imagine the communication officer informing the captain (program) about the status (pending, resolved, or rejected) of a message (Promise) from a distant outpost.

```javascript
requestSuppliesFromStarbase()
    .then(supplies => console.log("Received supplies: " + supplies)) // Resolved state (success)
    .catch(error => console.log("Supply request failed: " + error)); // Rejected state (error)
```

Benefits of Guaranteed Delivery

Error Handling

Promises allow you to handle successful results (resolved state) and errors (rejected state) in a structured way. Imagine the communication officer effectively relaying both successful messages and reporting any communication failures.

Chaining Operations

Promises can be chained together to handle sequences of asynchronous tasks. Imagine sending a request for supplies (Promise A), then using the received data (resolved state of Promise A) to update ship manifests (another asynchronous task handled by Promise B).

Async/Await

Async/await provides a cleaner way to write asynchronous code compared to traditional Promises. Think of your highly-organized first officer managing multiple asynchronous tasks (like sending messages and receiving data).

```javascript
// Traditional Promises (can be verbose)
requestSuppliesFromStarbase()
    .then(supplies => console.log("Received supplies: " + supplies))
    .catch(error => console.log("Supply request failed: " + error));

// Using async/await (cleaner syntax)
async function requestSupplies() {
    try {
        const supplies = await requestSuppliesFromStarbase();
        console.log("Received supplies: " + supplies);
    } catch (error) {
        console.log("Supply request failed: " + error);
    }
}

requestSupplies(); // Can be called like a regular function
console.log("Continuing with other ship operations...");
```

Awaiting Results

The `async` keyword marks a function as asynchronous. The `await` keyword pauses the execution of the function until a Promise is resolved (providing its data) or rejected (with an error). Imagine the pilot pausing ongoing tasks (like plotting a course) until a critical message (Promise) from a starbase is received (resolved) and its contents (supplies data) are available.

```javascript
async function receiveLandingInstructions() {
    const instructions = await requestLandingPermission();
    console.log("Landing instructions received: " + instructions);
    // Use the landing instructions here
}

receiveLandingInstructions(); // Awaits the Promise from requestLandingPermission
```

Benefits

Error Handling

Error handling remains an important aspect with `async/await`. You can use `try...catch` blocks to catch errors thrown from Promises within `await` expressions. Imagine the pilot anticipating potential issues (errors) and having contingency plans (error handling) in place.

Sequential Logic

`Async/await` can create a more intuitive flow for asynchronous operations, especially when dealing with chained Promises. Imagine the pilot handling tasks sequentially, waiting for each asynchronous step to complete before proceeding to the next.

Callback

Callbacks act like your ship's trusty crew members, relaying information and coordinating actions between different parts of your program.

Passing a Function

Callbacks are functions passed as arguments to other functions. The receiving function can then invoke the callback function at a later time, often after completing a task or receiving data. Think of a crew member (function) requesting information from a sensor station (another function) and providing a callback function (like a report) to receive the sensor data (information) once it's available.

```javascript
// Function requesting sensor data
function requestShieldStatus(callback) {
    setTimeout(() => {
        const shieldStrength = 85; // Simulate sensor reading
        callback(shieldStrength); // Invoke the callback function with data
    }, 1000); // Simulate a delay for sensor reading
}

// Callback function to receive shield data
function reportShieldStatus(strength) {
    console.log("Current shield strength: " + strength + "%");
}

requestShieldStatus(reportShieldStatus); // Pass the callback function
```

A Symphony of Actions (Asynchronous Communication)

Callbacks are particularly useful for handling asynchronous operations. The receiving function can continue with other tasks while waiting for the callback to be triggered with the results. Imagine the sensor station crew member (receiving function) being able to perform other maintenance tasks while waiting for the sensor reading to complete, and then notifying the bridge (callback function) with the data.

```javascript
function launchEscapePods(callback) {
    console.log("Initiating escape pod launch sequence...");
    setTimeout(() => {
        const launchStatus = "All escape pods launched successfully.";
        callback(launchStatus);
    }, 2000); // Simulate launch delay
}

function reportEscapePodStatus(message) {
    console.log(message);
}

launchEscapePods(reportEscapePodStatus); // Pass the callback function
console.log("Continuing with other evacuation procedures..."); // No waiting!
```

Working with APIs

The `"Fetch" API` acts like your ship's universal translator and communication device, enabling you to retrieve data from external sources seamlessly.

Making API Requests

The `fetch` API provides a modern and concise way to make HTTP requests to web servers and APIs (Application Programming Interfaces). Think of your ship using `fetch` to send a request (like asking for star chart data) to a friendly space station's API (web server) and receiving the response (star chart data) in a structured format.

```javascript
async function requestStarChartData() {
    const response = await fetch('https://galactic-navigation-api.com/star-charts');

    if (response.ok) { // Check for successful response
        const starChartData = await response.json(); // Parse JSON data
        console.log("Received star chart data:", starChartData);
    } else {
        console.log("Error fetching star chart data:", response.status);
    }
}

requestStarChartData();
```

A Wealth of Information at Your Fingertips (Data Retrieval)

`Fetch` allows you to retrieve data in various formats, such as JSON, text, or raw data streams. Imagine your ship using `fetch` to obtain detailed weather reports (JSON) from a nearby gas giant, download technical manuals (text) from an alien repository, or receive a live video feed (raw data stream) from a robotic probe exploring a distant nebula.

```javascript
async function downloadTechnicalManual(manualId) {
    const response = await fetch('https://alien-tech-archive.com/manuals/' + manualId);

    if (response.ok) {
        const manualData = await response.text(); // Download as text
        console.log("Downloaded technical manual:", manualData);
    } else {
        console.log("Error downloading technical manual:", response.status);
    }
}

downloadTechnicalManual('warp-drive-maintenance');
```

Benefits of Universal Communication

Simplified Data Fetching

`Fetch` offers a more concise and readable syntax compared to older methods like XMLHttpRequest for making HTTP requests.

Promise-Based Handling

`Fetch` utilizes Promises for asynchronous data retrieval, ensuring your program flow remains smooth while waiting for responses from external sources. Think of the ship's computer continuing with other tasks while its universal translator fetches data from a distant outpost.

Versatility

`Fetch` can handle various data formats and request methods (GET, POST, PUT, etc.), allowing you to interact with a wide range of external APIs.

This Keyword

this in a function

The "`this`" keyword acts like your ship's internal communication system, dynamically referencing the object that currently owns the function being executed.

Function Context

The value of `this` inside a function depends on how the function is called. In most cases, `this` refers to the object that the function is a method of. Think of a function specifically designed to control the ship's engines (method of the engine object). When this function is called from the engine object (like `engine.activateEngine()`), `this` inside the function will refer to the engine object itself.

```js
const engine = {
    powerLevel: 70,
    activateEngine: function() {
        console.log("Engines engaged at " + this.powerLevel + "% power.");
    }
};

engine.activateEngine(); // Outputs: "Engines engaged at 70% power." (this refers to engine object)
```

Function Calls

Imagine a general-purpose function for displaying messages on the ship's main screen (independent function). When called directly, the context of "this" inside the function won't refer to any specific object. The behavior of "this" can change depending on how a function is called. If a function is called independently (not as a method of an object), "this" within the function becomes the global object (usually window in a browser environment).

```javascript
function displayMessage(message) {
    console.log(this + ": " + message); // this might be the global object (window)
}

displayMessage("Shields online."); // Outputs: "[Window object]: Shields online."
```

```javascript
const navigationConsole = {
    location: "Deep Space Sector 14",
    displayLocation: function() {
        console.log("Current location: " + this.location);
    }
};

const reportLocation = navigationConsole.displayLocation; // Function reference (this undefined)
reportLocation(); // Outputs: "undefined: Current location: undefined" (this loses context)

reportLocation.call(navigationConsole); // Call with explicit this (navigationConsole)
// Outputs: "Current location: Deep Space Sector 14"
```

"this" in event handlers

The "this" keyword within event handlers acts like your ship's control interface, dynamically referencing the element that initiated the event.

Event Target

In event handlers (functions assigned to events like clicks or hover), "this" typically refers to the DOM element that triggered the event. Think of a function assigned to a button's click event (event handler). When the button is clicked, this inside the function will refer to the button element itself.

```javascript
const shieldsButton = document.getElementById("shieldsButton");

shieldsButton.addEventListener("click", function() {
    console.log(this); // Outputs: "<button id="shieldsButton">...</button>" (this refers to the button)
    console.log("Shields activated!");
});
```

Event Delegation

While this within event handlers often refers to the triggered element, event delegation allows you to attach a single event listener to a parent element and identify the specific child element that caused the event. Imagine having a central control panel (parent element) that monitors various buttons (child elements). You can use event delegation to identify which specific button was pressed (child element) when an event occurs on the control panel (parent element).

```html
<div id="controlPanel">
    <button id="weapon1Button">Fire Weapon 1</button>
    <button id="weapon2Button">Fire Weapon 2</button>
</div>
```

```javascript
const controlPanel = document.getElementById("controlPanel");

controlPanel.addEventListener("click", function(event) {
    if (event.target.id === "weapon1Button") {
        console.log("Weapon 1 fired!");
    } else if (event.target.id === "weapon2Button") {
        console.log("Weapon 2 fired!");
    }
});
```

Benefits of Responsive Controls

Event Delegation Efficiency

By understanding how "`this`" behaves with event delegation, you can reduce the number of event listeners needed and improve code maintainability. Imagine the control panel using a single event listener to handle clicks on both weapon buttons.

this in arrow functions

The "`this`" keyword within arrow functions behaves differently compared to regular functions, acting like your ship's unique communication protocol for these special functions.

Lexical this

Unlike regular functions where `this` depends on how the function is called, arrow functions have a different rule for "`this`". In arrow functions, "`this`" inherits the value of "`this`" from the surrounding lexical scope (the place where the arrow function is defined). Think of an arrow function created within a method of the engine object. Even if the arrow function is called independently, "`this`" inside the function will still refer to the engine object, just like its surrounding method.

```javascript
const engine = {
    powerLevel: 70,
    activateEngine: function() {
        const engageEngines = () => {
            console.log("Engines engaged at " + this.powerLevel + "% power.");
        };
        engageEngines(); // Outputs: "Engines engaged at 70% power." (this from engine object)
    }
};

engine.activateEngine();
```

Lexical Inheritance

This behavior of inheriting `this` from the surrounding scope allows arrow functions to maintain the context of the parent function. Imagine a series of nested arrow functions within the engine activation sequence. Each arrow function inherits `this` from the function where it's defined, ensuring they all refer to the engine object.

```javascript
const engine = {
    powerLevel: 70,
    activateEngine: () => {
        const engageEngines = () => {
            const prepareIgnition = () => {
                console.log("Engine preparing for ignition at " + this.powerLevel + "% power.");
            };
            prepareIgnition();
        };
        engageEngines();
    }
};

engine.activateEngine();   // Outputs: "Engine preparing for ignition at 70% power."
```

Benefits

Conciseness

Arrow functions often provide a cleaner syntax compared to traditional functions. The way `this` behaves within arrow functions aligns with this goal of conciseness, avoiding the need for explicit `this` binding in many cases. Imagine the engine control code being more streamlined using arrow functions.

Lexical Consistency

Inheriting `this` from the surrounding scope ensures consistent behavior within nested functions, making the code easier to reason about. Imagine the nested arrow functions within the engine activation sequence all clearly referring to the engine object.

"this" in a method

The "`this`" keyword within methods acts like your ship's internal communication system, dynamically referencing the object the method belongs to.

Object Context

When a method is called on an object, `this` inside the method refers to that specific object. Think of a method called `firePhasers` that exists on the weapons control object. When you call `weaponsControl.firePhasers()`, `this` inside the `firePhasers` method will refer to the `weaponsControl` object itself.

```javascript
const weaponsControl = {
    targetLocked: false,
    firePhasers: function() {
        if (this.targetLocked) {
            console.log("Phasers fired!");
        } else {
            console.log("No target locked, cannot fire phasers!");
        }
    }
};

weaponsControl.firePhasers(); // Outputs: "No target locked, cannot fire phasers!" (this refers to weaponsControl)
```

Method Calls

The "`this`" keyword allows methods to access the properties and other methods of the object they belong to. Imagine the `firePhasers` method needing to check the `targetLocked` property (of the `weaponsControl` object) before firing. Using `this.targetLocked`, the method can access this information directly.

```
weaponsControl.targetLocked = true;
weaponsControl.firePhasers(); // Outputs: "Phasers fired!" (this refers to weaponsControl)
```

Benefits of Contextual Control

Object-Oriented Design: The "this" keyword is a fundamental concept in object-oriented programming, allowing methods to operate on the data and functionality specific to their object. Imagine having separate phaser banks (objects) at the front and back of your ship, each with their own `firePhasers` method. The "this" keyword ensures each method works with the phaser bank it belongs to.

Code Readability: By using `this`, code becomes more readable as it clarifies which object's properties or methods are being used within the method. Imagine the `firePhasers` method clearly indicating it's checking the `targetLocked` property of the current `weaponsControl` object.

Modules

Modules allow you to organize your JavaScript code into reusable and self-contained units. Think of separate modules for the warp core, phaser banks, and life support systems. Each module would contain all the functions and variables specific to that system.

```js
// warpCore.js (Module for warp core functionality)
export function engageWarpDrive() {
    console.log("Engaging warp drive!");
}

export function disengageWarpDrive() {
    console.log("Disengaging warp drive.");
}

```

Modular Construction (Import and Export)

Modules can export specific functions or variables that you can then import and use in other parts of your program. Imagine the navigation module needing to call the `engageWarpDrive` function from the warp core module. It can import this function using the `import` statement.

```javascript
// navigation.js (Module for navigation functionality)
import { engageWarpDrive } from './warpCore.js'; // Import function from warpCore.js

function setCourse(destination) {
    console.log("Setting course for: " + destination);
    engageWarpDrive(); // Use imported function
}

setCourse("Starbase Alpha");
```

DOM Manipulation

DOM manipulation allows you to dynamically modify the structure, content, and style of the web page (your starship's bridge interface) to reflect the state of your vessel and crew.

Document Object Model

The DOM is a hierarchical representation of web page content, comprising elements like buttons and paragraphs. Manipulating the DOM with JavaScript involves updating values on displays or changing button functions.

DOM Selection and Modification

JavaScript provides various methods to select and modify elements within the DOM:

getElementById

Retrieves an element by its unique ID (like finding a specific control panel on the bridge).

getElementsByClassName

Retrieves a collection of elements with the same class name (like selecting all the status displays).

querySelector

Selects the first element that matches a CSS selector (like targeting a specific button with a unique class).

Once you have a reference to an element, you can use methods like:

textContent

Change the text content of an element (like updating a display with a new value).

innerHTML

Modify the entire HTML content within an element (like creating a more complex status report).

style

Change the style properties of an element (like altering the color of an alert light).

```javascript
const shieldStatusDisplay = document.getElementById("shieldStatus");
shieldStatusDisplay.textContent = "Shields: Online (75%)"; // Update shield status

const warningLight = document.querySelector(".warning-light");
warningLight.style.backgroundColor = "red"; // Turn on warning light

```

Benefits

Dynamic User Interfaces: DOM manipulation enables interactive interfaces that respond to user actions and update based on program logic, such as automatically adjusting shield status displays as damage occurs.

Real-Time Feedback: By manipulating the DOM, you can offer real-time feedback to the crew about the ship's system status, like flashing red lights and warning messages appearing when hull integrity drops.

Data Visualization: DOM manipulation techniques create dynamic data visualizations like progress bars or animated gauges, representing complex information, such as a status display filling up with green bars as the ship approaches its destination.

Type Checkers - TypeScript

TypeScript vs JavaScript

JavaScript

JavaScript (JS) is similar, offering a flexible and versatile scripting language for building web applications.

TypeScript

TypeScript (TS) acts like an engineer's toolkit, building upon JavaScript and adding features that make code more robust and maintainable.

Choosing the Right Crew for the Mission

Starting a new project

If you're embarking on a new and unexplored mission (web application), JavaScript might be a good choice due to its ease of use and rapid prototyping capabilities. It allows you to get your core functionality up and running quickly.

Maintaining a large codebase

For extensive missions involving constant expansion and maintenance of a large codebase (such as a complex web application), TypeScript may be preferable. With features like type checking and static analysis, it serves as blueprints for your system, detecting potential issues early and ensuring a smoother journey.

TS Playground

What is the TS Playground?

It's like your ship's holodeck for TypeScript training! Engineers can write and test TypeScript code without setting up a complex development environment.

Why use it

Quick learning: Experiment and see results instantly, perfect for understanding TypeScript basics. Testing ideas: Try out new features or troubleshoot code snippets before using them in your main project. Collaboration: Easily share code examples to help other crew members. It's a simulator, not your full ship. For building real Typescript applications, you'll need a proper development setup; we will look into that in the React section of this book.

Start Playing!

Head to the TypeScript Playground (search "TypeScript Lang Playground") on Google and start experimenting to master your TypeScript skills!

Tsconfig.json

The `tsconfig.json` file acts like your chief engineer's manual for TypeScript, specifying how the compiler should interpret and process your code for your application. By default, TypeScript comes with a basic configuration.This default configuration works for simple projects, but for complex applications, you might want to fine-tune these settings to optimize the compilation process.

```
// Basic tsconfig.json (simplified)
{
    "compilerOptions": {}
}
```

Customizing the Compiler

The `tsconfig.json` file lets you customize various compiler options. Imagine equipping your engineering team with a detailed manual that explains how to adjust the ship's engines, shields, and other systems for optimal performance. These compiler options let you define how TypeScript should handle aspects like target JavaScript version (ES5, ES6+), type checking strictness, and module system (CommonJS, ES Modules).

```json
{
    "compilerOptions": {
        "target": "es2015", // Generate JavaScript code compatible with ES6
        "strict": true, // Enable stricter type checking
        "module": "esnext", // Use ES Modules for code organization
        // ... other options
    }
}
```

```json
{
    "compilerOptions": {
        // ... other options
    },
    "include": ["src/**/*.ts"], // Include all TypeScript files in the 'src' directory
    "exclude": ["node_modules", "**/*.test.ts"] // Exclude node_modules and test files
}
```

Typescript Types

The Perils of Loose Coupling (JavaScript and Unexpected Data)

Traditional JavaScript uses loose typing, meaning variables can hold different data types throughout the code. This can lead to errors if you accidentally try to perform mathematical operations on a string value instead of a number.

```javascript
// JavaScript (simplified example)
let shieldStrength = 100; // Number
shieldStrength = "partially operational"; // String (unexpected data type)
```

Defining Data Types with TypeScript

TypeScript introduces the concept of types, which act like technical specifications for your system. By explicitly defining types for variables and function arguments, TypeScript ensures data consistency and helps catch errors early in development.

```typescript
// TypeScript (simplified example)
let shieldStrength: number = 100; // Define variable type as number

function firePhasers(power: number): string {
    // Enforces power argument to be a number
    return `Phasers fired at ${power} power!`;
}
```

```typescript
let shieldStrength: number = 100;
shieldStrength = "partially operational"; // TypeScript compiler error!

function firePhasers(power: string): string { // Error: power argument should be a number
    return `Phasers fired at ${power} power!`;
}
```

Type Inference

Type inference acts like your ship's intuitive and efficient construction supervisor, analyzing existing code and automatically determining the data types of variables and function arguments, streamlining development for your crew.

```
// Traditional JavaScript (simplified example)
let hullMaterial: string = "durasteel";
let enginePower: number = 100;

function activateShields(strength: number): void {
    // ... function logic
}

```

Type Inference to the Rescue

TypeScript introduces type inference, a powerful feature that allows the compiler to automatically deduce the data type of a variable or function argument based on its assignment or usage. Imagine your engineering supervisor observing the construction process and based on the materials being used (durasteel) and the assigned value (100), they can infer that the hullMaterial variable is a string and enginePower is a number. This eliminates the need for explicit type definitions in many cases.

```typescript
// TypeScript with type inference (simplified example)
let hullMaterial = "durasteel"; // Type inferred as string
let enginePower = 100; // Type inferred as number

function activateShields(strength: number): void {
    // ... function logic
}

```

```typescript
let alienArtifact: any; // Inferred as 'any' (unknown type)

alienArtifact = "unknown material"; // Type remains 'any'
alienArtifact = 42; // Type inference might not update due to previous assignment

// Use annotation for clarity
let alienArtifactReading: string = "unknown material (needs further analysis)";

```

Function Overloading

Function overloading acts like your ship's multi-purpose control panels, allowing you to define functions with the same name but different parameter lists, enabling them to handle various scenarios efficiently. Imagine equipping your bridge with a single phaser control panel that can handle different phaser types. By overloading the `firePhasers` function, you can specify separate parameter lists for power level only (generic phasers) or power level and phaser type (red or blue phasers). The compiler intelligently determines which function definition to use based on the arguments provided during the call.

```javascript
// Traditional JavaScript (simplified example)
function firePhasers(powerLevel) {
    console.log(`Firing phasers at ${powerLevel} power!`);
}

// Need separate functions for different phaser types
function fireRedPhasers(powerLevel) {
    console.log(`Firing red phasers at ${powerLevel} power!`);
}

function fireBluePhasers(powerLevel) {
    console.log(`Firing blue phasers at ${powerLevel} power!`);
}
```

```typescript
// TypeScript function overloading (simplified example)
function firePhasers(powerLevel: number): void;
function firePhasers(powerLevel: number, phaserType: string): void;

function firePhasers(powerLevel: number, phaserType?: string) {
    if (phaserType) {
        console.log(`Firing ${phaserType} phasers at ${powerLevel} power!`);
    } else {
        console.log(`Firing phasers at ${powerLevel} power!`);
    }
}

// Usage examples
firePhasers(75); // Generic phasers
firePhasers(50, "red"); // Red phasers
```

```typescript
function activateShields(shieldStrength: number): string; // Returns shield status message
function activateShields(weaponType: string): boolean; // Returns true if weapon systems online

function activateShields(argument: number | string): string | boolean {
    // ... function logic based on argument type
}

```

Namespaces

Namespaces act like your ship's compartmentalization system, allowing you to group related functions, classes, variables, and constants within a designated namespace, preventing naming conflicts and promoting code organization. Imagine equipping your engineers with designated compartments (namespaces) on each deck (file) to store related systems and components. Namespaces provide a way to group functions, classes, variables, and constants under a specific name, preventing conflicts with identically named elements from other parts of your codebase.

```
// Global scope (simplified example)
function calculateEnginePower(warpFactor) {
    // ... engine power calculation logic
}

const bridgeAlert = "Warning: Incoming enemy vessel!";

function fireWeapons(target) {
    // ... weapons firing logic
}
```

```typescript
// Namespaces (simplified example)
namespace Starship {
    export function calculateEnginePower(warpFactor: number): number {
        // ... engine power calculation logic
    }

    export const bridgeAlert = "Warning: Incoming enemy vessel!";

    export function fireWeapons(target: string): void {
        // ... weapons firing logic
    }
}

// Accessing namespaced elements
const enginePower = Starship.calculateEnginePower(5);
console.log(Starship.bridgeAlert);
Starship.fireWeapons("enemy cruiser");
```

Conflicting Names and Access Modifiers

Imagine encountering another starship with similar systems but named identically (e.g., `fireWeapons`). Namespaces prevent these conflicts by isolating elements within their respective scopes. Additionally, you can use access modifiers (public, private) within namespaces to control the visibility of elements from other parts of your codebase.

```typescript
namespace Starship {
    export function firePhasers(target: string): void {
        // ... phaser firing logic
    }

    // Private function not accessible outside the namespace
    private function initiateWarpDrive() {
        // ... warp drive logic
    }
}

// Only firePhasers is accessible from outside the Starship namespace
Starship.firePhasers("enemy fighter");
```

Classes

Building from Scratch (Traditional JavaScript Objects)

Traditionally, in JavaScript, objects are used to represent real-world entities with properties (data) and methods (functions). Imagine your engineers building starship components piece by piece, defining properties like `weaponType` and methods like `fire` directly on individual objects. This approach can work for simple components, but it becomes cumbersome and error-prone for complex systems with repeated functionalities.

```javascript
// Traditional JavaScript object (simplified example)
const phaserBank = {
    weaponType: "phaser",
    fire: function () {
        console.log("Firing phasers!");
    },
};

const photonTorpedoLauncher = {
    weaponType: "photon torpedo",
    fire: function () {
        console.log("Launching photon torpedo!");
    },
};
```

TypeScript Classes

TypeScript introduces classes, a powerful concept in object-oriented programming. Imagine equipping your engineers with detailed blueprints (classes) that define the structure and behavior of starship components. These blueprints can be used to create multiple instances (objects) of the component, each inheriting the properties and methods defined in the class. This promotes code reusability and maintainability.

```typescript
// TypeScript class (simplified example)
class Weapon {
    constructor(public readonly weaponType: string) {}

    fire(): void {
        console.log(`Firing ${this.weaponType} weapon!`);
    }
}

// Creating weapon instances
const phaserBank = new Weapon("phaser");
const photonTorpedoLauncher = new Weapon("photon torpedo");

phaserBank.fire(); // Output: Firing phaser weapon!
photonTorpedoLauncher.fire(); // Output: Firing photon torpedo weapon!
```

Constructors, Inheritance, and Polymorphism

Imagine needing a new type of weapon, a rapid-fire phaser bank. Constructors are used to initialize properties when creating a new object (weapon instance). Inheritance allows you to create specialized classes (like RapidFirePhaserBank) that inherit properties and methods from a base class (Weapon). Polymorphism enables objects of different classes (phaserBank, photonTorpedoLauncher, rapidFirePhaserBank) to respond differently to the same method call (fire).

```
class RapidFirePhaserBank extends Weapon {
    constructor() {
        super("rapid-fire phaser"); // Call base class constructor
    }

    fire(): void {
        console.log("Firing phasers in rapid succession!");
    }
}

const rapidFirePhaserBank = new RapidFirePhaserBank();
rapidFirePhaserBank.fire(); // Output: Firing phasers in rapid succession!
```

Tsc

What is TSC?

TSC is the TypeScript Compiler. It's your warp drive engineer's translator, taking TypeScript blueprints and turning them into JavaScript code that your web-app can run.

Why use it?

Automation

No more translating code by hand! TSC makes development faster and less error-prone.

Type Safety

TSC enforces your TypeScript rules, catching potential bugs before things go boom.

Integration

Works seamlessly with your project setup for a smooth workflow.

How to use it (simplified)

1. Write TypeScript in `.ts` files.
2. Run `tsc <filename>.ts` in your terminal.
3. TSC spits out a runnable `.js` file!

Server Side Rendering - React

Vite

Vite acts like your ship's revolutionary new replicator, accelerating development workflows by providing an innovative approach to building and serving React applications. Imagine equipping your engineers with Vite. It utilizes a unique approach that leverages browser APIs for on-demand module transformation, eliminating the need for pre-bundling during development. This results in blazing-fast hot module replacement (HMR), allowing your engineers to see changes in the browser almost instantly as they code.

Traditional Development Workflow

Traditional workflow steps (simplified)

1. Write React code

2. Run a build command to compile code and bundle resources

3. Refresh the browser to see changes

Vite to the Rescue

Development workflow with Vite (simplified)

1. Write React code

2. See changes reflected in the browser nearly instantly!

Development Server and Bundling for Production

Imagine needing to simulate a real-world environment for testing before deploying your starship (application) to space (production). Vite provides a development server that mimics a production setup, allowing for comprehensive testing. When it's time for launch, Vite can generate optimized production builds for deployment.

Creating a React Application With Vite

Prerequisites

Node.js and npm: Ensure you have Node.js and npm installed on your system. These tools act as the foundation for building your React application. You can check their installation by running `node -v` and `npm -v` in your terminal.

VS Code: Have VS Code Editor, ready for action.

Project Initialization

- Open Terminal: Launch your terminal application.
- Navigate: Use the cd command to navigate to your desired project directory.
- Summon the Vite CLI: Execute the following command to create a new React project with TypeScript support: `npm init vite@latest my-react-app --template react-ts`
- Replace `my-react-app` with your preferred project name. This command utilizes the Vite CLI (command-line interface) and the `react-ts` template to set up a project structure optimized for React and TypeScript.

VS Code Integration

Open the Project: Once the initialization is complete, open the newly created project directory in VS Code. You can usually do this by dragging the folder onto the VS Code icon.

TypeScript Configuration: VS Code should automatically detect TypeScript files and offer IntelliSense (code completion) features. If not, ensure you have the "Typescript" extension installed in VS Code.

Project Structure

src: This folder contains your React components and application logic written in TypeScript files. public: This folder holds static assets like images or favicons. index.html: The main HTML file that serves as the entry point for your React application. main.tsx: The primary TypeScript file where your React application's root component is defined. vite.config.ts: The configuration file for Vite, customizing build and development settings.

Running the Application

Open Terminal (Again): Open the terminal within VS Code (usually located at the bottom panel).

Start the Development Server: Run the following command to start the development server: `npm run dev`

This will launch a local development server, typically accessible at http://localhost:3000/ in your web browser. You should see your React application running! With this basic setup, you have a React application with TypeScript support running on Vite in VS Code. Now you can explore creating components, handling user interactions, and building a fully-fledged React application using the power of TypeScript!

Additional Tips

Explore the official Vite documentation (https://vitejs.dev/) for more in-depth configuration options and functionalities. Utilize VS Code extensions like "React Snippets" or "ESLint" to enhance your development experience with React and TypeScript.

React Components

React components are reusable building blocks that create the UI of your web application. Think of a component like a blueprint for a specific section of the ship's interface, such as an engine control panel or a sensor display. These components can be customized with props and state to create a dynamic and interactive UI. TSX acts like blueprints for components, allowing you to combine the flexibility of JavaScript with the type safety and code organization of TypeScript.

```
function EngineControlPanel(props) {
    // JSX to define the component's structure and behavior
    return (
        <div>
            {/* UI elements for engine controls here */}
        </div>
    );
}
```

Benefits of TSX

TSX allows you to write HTML-like syntax within Typescript code. This makes it easier to create the structure of your React components. Imagine having pre-defined components for warp core displays, thruster controls, and other frequently used UI elements.

More importantly, TSX leverages the power of TypeScript, a superset of JavaScript that adds optional static typing. Think of adding labels and specifications to your blueprints to ensure components are built correctly. TypeScript helps catch errors early in the development process by enforcing data types for props, state variables, and function arguments.

```typescript
interface EngineProps {
    warpCoreTemperature: number; // Define the type of prop expected by EngineControlPanel
    onEngineStart: () => void; // Define the type of function expected for the event handler
}

function EngineControlPanel(props: EngineProps) {
    const { warpCoreTemperature, onEngineStart } = props;

    return (
        <div>
            Warp Core Temperature: {warpCoreTemperature} C
            <button onClick={onEngineStart}>Engage Warp Drive</button>
        </div>
    );
}
```

```
interface WarpCoreState {
    isEngaged: boolean;
}

function WarpCore(props: EngineProps, state: WarpCoreState) {
    // ... component logic using props and state with types
}
```

Components and Communication

React components are reusable building blocks that create the UI of your web application. Think of the bridge as a component, containing smaller components like control panels, status displays, and communication stations. These components work together to provide a unified user interface.

Props (Incoming Data)

Imagine various systems on the ship sending data (props) to the bridge. Props are external properties passed down from parent components to child components. They provide a way for child components to receive data and instructions from their parents. For example, a sensor panel component might receive a prop named `shieldStrength` from its parent component to display the current shield status.

```jsx
// Parent Component (Sending Props)
function Bridge() {
    const shieldStrength = 80; // Bridge has internal knowledge of shield status
    return (
        <div>
            <SensorPanel shieldStrength={shieldStrength} />  {/* Passing shieldStrength as a prop */}
        </div>
    );
}

// Child Component (Receiving Props)
function SensorPanel(props) {
    const incomingShieldStrength = props.shieldStrength;  // Access prop value
    return (
        <div>Shield Strength: {incomingShieldStrength}%</div>
    );
}
```

State (Internal Management)

Imagine the bridge having its own internal displays and controls specific to its function. State is managed within a component itself and allows it to react to user interactions or internal changes. It represents the component's own data and can be updated. For example, the bridge might have a state variable for the current course (`course`) that can be changed by the helmsman using UI controls.

```jsx
function Bridge() {
    const [course, setCourse] = useState("Alpha Centauri");  // State variable for course

    const updateCourse = (newCourse) => {
        setCourse(newCourse);  // Update state using a function
    };

    return (
        <div>
            <Heading course={course} />  {/* Passing course as a prop */}
            <CourseControl updateCourse={updateCourse} />  {/* Passing updateCourse function as a prop */}
        </div>
    );
}

// Child Component (Using State)
function Heading(props) {
    const currentCourse = props.course;
    return (
        <h1>Current Course: {currentCourse}</h1>
    );
}

// Child Component (Updating State)
function CourseControl(props) {
    const handleCourseChange = (event) => {
        props.updateCourse(event.target.value);  // Call parent's function to update state
    };

    return (
        <input type="text" onChange={handleCourseChange} placeholder="Enter New Course" />
    );
}
```

When to Use Props vs State

Use props to pass data down from parent to child components and for data that needs to be shared across multiple components. Imagine the captain receiving sensor data (prop) about an enemy ship from a long-range scanner component and then passing that data (prop) to the weapons control component to target the enemy.

Use state to manage data specific to a component and its behavior. Imagine the weapons control component having its own state variable for the number of phaser torpedoes remaining, which is independent of other components.

Conditional Rendering

Conditional rendering acts like your control panels, allowing you to dynamically show or hide UI elements based on specific conditions.

JSX and Components

React uses JSX (JavaScript XML) to create a declarative style for building UI components. Think of your bridge layout being constructed from reusable components like status displays, weapon control panels, and navigation charts. Each component controls a specific section of the UI.

```
1  function BridgeDisplay() {
2      return (
3          <div>
4              {/* Various UI elements here */}
5          </div>
6      );
7  }
8
```

Conditional Statements - if/else

React offers conditional statements like `if` and `else` to control which UI elements are rendered based on JavaScript expressions (conditions). Imagine a phaser control panel that only displays the "Fire" button if a target is locked (true condition).

```
1  function PhaserControlPanel(props) {
2      const targetLocked = props.targetLocked; // Get target lock status from props
3
4      if (targetLocked) {
5          return <button>Fire Phasers!</button>;
6      } else {
7          return <p>Targeting enemy ship...</p>;
8      }
9  }
10
```

Ternary Operator

React also provides the ternary operator (`condition ? expressionIfTrue : expressionIfFalse`) for concise conditional rendering. Imagine a warp core status display that shows "Warp Drive Engaged" when active or "Warp Drive Offline" otherwise.

```
1  function WarpCoreDisplay(props) {
2      const warpDriveActive = props.warpDriveActive;
3
4      return (
5          <div>
6              Warp Core: {warpDriveActive ? "Engaged" : "Offline"}
7          </div>
8      );
9  }
```

Logical Operators

Imagine a warning message that appears only if the shields are failing (condition 1) AND the hull integrity is below 20% (condition 2).

```
function WarningDisplay(props) {
    const shieldsFailing = props.shieldsFailing;
    const hullIntegrity = props.hullIntegrity;

    if (shieldsFailing && hullIntegrity < 20) {
        return (
            <div className="warning">Warning! Critical damage detected!</div>
        );
    }

    return null; // Don't render anything if conditions not met
}
```

Rendering

Lists and Keys

React's Rendering with Lists and Keys acts like your crew manifest system, ensuring each crew member is displayed efficiently and uniquely identifiable.

React Lists

React allows you to render lists of elements efficiently. Think of the crew manifest being a list containing information about each crew member, like name, rank, and department. You can use JSX to iterate through this list and display each member's information individually.

```jsx
const crewManifest = [
    { name: "Captain James T. Kirk", rank: "Captain", department: "Command" },
    { name: "Spock", rank: "Commander", department: "Science" },
    { name: "Uhura", rank: "Lieutenant", department: "Communications" },
];

function CrewManifestDisplay() {
    return (
        <ul>
            {crewManifest.map((crewMember) => (
                <li key={crewMember.name}>  {/* Temporary placeholder for key */}
                    {/* Display crew member information here */}
                </li>
            ))}
        </ul>
    );
}
```

Avoiding Identity Crisis (The Importance of Keys)

When rendering lists, it's crucial to assign a unique identifier (key) to each item. Imagine accidentally assigning the same ID badge to multiple crew members, causing confusion! Keys act like unique ID badges for each crew member in the list. They help React identify which items have changed, been added, or removed, allowing for efficient updates to the UI.

```
function CrewManifestDisplay() {
    return (
        <ul>
            {crewManifest.map((crewMember) => (
                <li key={crewMember.id}> {/* Use a unique ID property for the key */}
                    Name: {crewMember.name} - Rank: {crewMember.rank}
                </li>
            ))}
        </ul>
    );
}
```

It's generally recommended to use a unique property from your data (like an ID) as the key. Avoid using the index of the item in the array as a key, as this can lead to issues if the order of the list changes.

Beam Up New Crew Members (Efficient Updates with Keys)

Keys enable React to optimize rendering performance when lists change. Imagine adding a new crew member to the manifest. With proper keys, React can efficiently update the UI to display the new member without re-rendering the entire list.

```js
// Adding a new crew member to the manifest
crewManifest.push({ name: "Dr. McCoy", rank: "Lieutenant Commander", department: "Medical" });
```

Hooks

React's `useReducer` hook acts like your ship's central control unit, allowing you to handle intricate state updates and logic in a modular and organized way.

Traditional State Management

React traditionally uses the `useState` hook for managing component state. Think of individual ship systems like shields or phasers using `useState` to track their current power levels or operational status (on/off). This approach can work well for simple components, but it can become cumbersome for complex state logic with multiple interconnected values.

```
1  function PhasersControl() {
2      const [phaserPower, setPhaserPower] = useState(50); // Phaser
   power level state
3
4      const increasePhaserPower = () => {
5          setPhaserPower(phaserPower + 10); // Update power level
6      };
7
8      return (
9          <div>
10             Phaser Power: {phaserPower}%
11             <button onClick={increasePhaserPower}>Increase
   Power</button>
12         </div>
13     );
14 }
```

Introducing useReducer

`useReducer` provides an alternative for managing complex state with multiple sub-values and intricate update logic. Imagine having a central core that controls multiple subsystems and their interactions. `useReducer` allows you to define a reducer function that encapsulates the state update logic for your entire system.

```javascript
function reducer(state, action) {
    switch (action.type) {
        case "INCREASE_PHASER_POWER":
            return { ...state, phaserPower: state.phaserPower + 10 };
        case "SHIELD_HIT":
            return { ...state, shieldStrength: state.shieldStrength - action.damage };
        default:
            return state;
    }
}

function StarshipCore() {
    const initialState = { phaserPower: 50, shieldStrength: 80 };
    const [state, dispatch] = useReducer(reducer, initialState);

    const increasePhaserPower = () => {
        dispatch({ type: "INCREASE_PHASER_POWER" });
    };

    const takeShieldHit = (damage) => {
        dispatch({ type: "SHIELD_HIT", damage });
    };

    return (
        <div>
            <PhasersControl phaserPower={state.phaserPower} increasePower={increasePhaserPower} />
            <ShieldsDisplay shieldStrength={state.shieldStrength} takeHit={takeShieldHit} />
        </div>
    );
}

function PhasersControl(props) {
    // ... uses props for phaserPower and increasePower function
}

function ShieldsDisplay(props) {
    // ... uses props for shieldStrength and takeHit function
}
```

```
function reducer(state, action) {
    // ... existing logic
    case "INCREASE_PHASER_POWER":
        if (state.shieldStrength > 20) {
            return { ...state, phaserPower: state.phaserPower + 10 };
        } else {
            return state; // Don't increase power if shields are low
        }
}
```

useMemo

The `useMemo` hook acts like a caching engineer, optimizing performance by ensuring expensive calculations are only done when necessary.

Traditional Functions and Performance

React components can call functions that perform calculations or data manipulation. Imagine a function that calculates the optimal warp core efficiency based on current engine power and coolant levels. While this function is useful, calling it repeatedly during rendering can be inefficient, especially if the input values haven't changed.

```jsx
function EngineControlPanel(props) {
    const enginePower = props.enginePower;
    const coolantLevel = props.coolantLevel;

    const calculateEfficiency = () => {
        // Complex calculation based on enginePower and coolantLevel
        return efficiencyValue;
    };

    const efficiency = calculateEfficiency();

    return (
        <div>
            Warp Core Efficiency: {efficiency}%
        </div>
    );
}
```

Memoization with useMemo

`useMemo` allows you to memorize function call results. Imagine your engineer realizing a specific calculation is being performed repeatedly with the same inputs. Memoization is like storing the result of a complex calculation with a specific input set, so you don't have to perform the calculation again if the inputs haven't changed.

```javascript
function EngineControlPanel(props) {
    const enginePower = props.enginePower;
    const coolantLevel = props.coolantLevel;

    const calculateEfficiency = useMemo(() => {
        // Complex calculation based on enginePower and coolantLevel
        return efficiencyValue;
    }, [enginePower, coolantLevel]); // Re-calculate only if enginePower or coolantLevel changes

    const efficiency = calculateEfficiency;

    return (
        <div>
            Warp Core Efficiency: {efficiency}%
        </div>
    );
}
```

useMemo and Component Updates

Remember that `useMemo` only guarantees the function is not called again if the dependency array values (like `enginePower` and `coolantLevel` in our example) haven't changed. If these values change, the function will be re-run to compute a new result.

Basic hooks

useState

React's `useState` hook acts like your control panels, allowing you to manage the state (data) of your components and update the UI accordingly.

Components and State

Think of your bridge as a React component, containing smaller components for specific functions, like a tactical display, shield status panel, and navigation console. Each component can have its own state to manage the information it displays.

```jsx
function Bridge() {
    // State variables to hold data for the bridge
    const [shieldStrength, setShieldStrength] = useState(80); // Shield strength percentage
    const [course, setCourse] = useState("Alpha Centauri"); // Current course

    // ... component logic and UI elements using state and functions to update it
    return (
        <div>
            <ShieldDisplay shieldStrength={shieldStrength} />  {/* Pass shield data as a prop */}
            <NavigationConsole course={course} updateCourse={setCourse} />  {/* Pass course data and update function as props */}
        </div>
    );
}
```

Updating State

`useState` returns an array with two elements: the current state value and a function to update it. Imagine the tactical officer reporting incoming fire, causing the shield strength to decrease. You can use the function returned by `useState` (here, `setShieldStrength`) to update the shield strength state variable.

```
function Bridge() {
    // ... existing component logic

    const takeShieldHit = (damage) => {
        setShieldStrength(shieldStrength - damage); // Update shield strength based on damage taken
    };

    return (
        <div>
            {/* ... existing UI elements */}
            <WarningLights takeHit={takeShieldHit} />  {/* Pass takeShieldHit function as a prop */}
        </div>
    );
}

function WarningLights(props) {
    const handleHit = () => {
        props.takeHit(10); // Simulate shield hit with 10 points of damage
    };

    return (
        <button onClick={handleHit}>Enemy Fire Incoming!</button>
    );
}
```

State and User Interaction

Imagine the pilot needing to update the ship's course. You can use state to store the current course and provide a way for the user (the pilot) to change it through an input field or buttons.

```javascript
function NavigationConsole(props) {
    const updateCourse = props.updateCourse; // Function to update course state from Bridge

    const handleCourseChange = (event) => {
        updateCourse(event.target.value); // Update course state using function passed as a prop
    };

    return (
        <div>
            Current Course: {props.course}
            <input type="text" onChange={handleCourseChange} placeholder="Enter New Course" />
        </div>
    );
}
```

useEffect

React's `useEffect` hook acts like your crew automation protocols, allowing you to execute side effects in functional components based on certain conditions.

Components and Side Effects

React components are reusable building blocks that create the UI. Think of various sections of your ship as components, like an engine monitor, a sensor grid display, or a communication console. These components may need to perform actions beyond rendering the UI, such as fetching data from the ship's computer or subscribing to sensor updates. These are considered side effects.

```
function EngineMonitor() {
    // ... JSX to display engine data

    return (
        <div>
            {/* Engine data display elements */}
        </div>
    );
}
```

useEffect for Side Effects

useEffect allows you to run side effects within functional components. Imagine needing the engine monitor to automatically fetch and display the latest engine data from the ship's computer core upon initial render. useEffect provides a way to hook into the component lifecycle and execute this side effect at the appropriate time.

```javascript
function SensorGrid() {
    const [sensorData, setSensorData] = useState([]); // State to hold sensor readings

    useEffect(() => {
        // Subscribe to sensor data feed on component mount
        const subscription = navigator.sensor.watch(sensorType, (data) => {
            setSensorData(data.readings);
        });

        // Cleanup function to unsubscribe on component unmount (prevents memory leaks)
        return () => subscription.unsubscribe();
    }, []); // Empty dependency array: run effect only on mount and cleanup on unmount

    return (
        <div>
            {/* Display latest sensor readings */}
        </div>
    );
}
```

useEffect for Data Subscriptions

Imagine needing the sensor grid to continuously update with the latest readings from the ship's scanners. You can use useEffect to establish a subscription to the sensor data feed and update the UI accordingly.

Following Orders (useEffect Dependency Array)

The second argument to `useEffect` is an optional dependency array. This array specifies which values the effect should depend on. Imagine needing the engine monitor to refetch data only when a specific engine parameter selection component (prop) changes on the bridge. You can include that prop in the dependency array to re-run the data fetching logic whenever the selection changes.

```
function EngineMonitor(props) {
    const selectedEngineParameter = props.selectedParameter; // Prop for engine parameter selection

    useEffect(() => {
        // ... existing data fetching logic
    }, [selectedEngineParameter]); // Re-run effect only when selectedParameter prop changes
}
```

Routing - React Router

React Router acts like your ship's navigation system, allowing you to define routes for different parts of your UI and transition between them seamlessly.

Components and Navigation

Think of different sections of your ship as components, like a bridge component, an engine control component, and a crew roster component. React Router helps you organize these components and navigate between them based on the user's actions (like clicking buttons or following links).

```jsx
// Bridge Component
function Bridge() {
    return (
        <div>
            {/* UI elements for the bridge */}
            <button onClick={() => navigate("/engine")}>Go to Engineering</button>
        </div>
    );
}

// Engine Control Component
function EngineControl() {
    return (
        <div>
            {/* UI elements for engine controls */}
            <button onClick={() => navigate("/crew")}>View Crew Roster</button>
        </div>
    );
}

// Crew Roster Component
function CrewRoster() {
    return (
        <div>
            {/* UI elements for crew roster */}
        </div>
    );
}
```

Routing with React Router

React Router provides components and hooks to manage routing within your React application. Imagine installing a navigation system on your ship that displays the current location (URL path) and allows the crew to travel to different sections using buttons or menus. React Router integrates with your components to handle these navigation actions.

```
import { BrowserRouter as Router, Routes, Route, useNavigate } from "react-router-dom";

function App() {
    return (
        <Router>
            <Routes>
                <Route path="/" element={<Bridge />} />
                <Route path="/engine" element={<EngineControl />} />
                <Route path="/crew" element={<CrewRoster />} />
            </Routes>
        </Router>
    );
}
```

In this example

- A `Router` component from React Router Dom is used to wrap the application.
- `Routes` component defines the available routes.
- Each `Route` component specifies a path (URL) and the corresponding component to render for that path.

Exploring the Holodeck (Dynamic Routing with Parameters)

Imagine having a crew roster component that can display information for a specific crew member. You can define routes with URL parameters to achieve this dynamic behavior.

```
function CrewMember(props) {
    const crewMemberId = props.match.params.id; // Access parameter from URL path
    // ... logic to fetch and display crew member information based on ID
    return (
        <div>
            {/* Crew member details */}
        </div>
    );
}

<Route path="/crew/:id" element={<CrewMember />} /> {/* Route with parameter for crew member ID */}
```

Styling

React MUI acts like your ship's chief designer, providing a comprehensive set of pre-built and customizable React components that adhere to Google's Material Design principles.

Traditional UI Development

Traditionally, building UIs from scratch involves writing a lot of CSS and component logic. Imagine your engineers spending a significant amount of time designing and implementing individual buttons, menus, dialogs, and other UI elements. This can lead to design inconsistencies and require a lot of repetitive code.

```javascript
// Button component (simplified example)
function Button({ label, onClick }) {
    const styles = {
        backgroundColor: 'blue',
        color: 'white',
        padding: '10px 20px',
        borderRadius: '5px',
        cursor: 'pointer',
    };

    return (
        <button style={styles} onClick={onClick}>{label}</button>
    );
}
```

React MUI

React MUI (Material-UI) is a popular library for building user interfaces with React components based on Material Design. Imagine equipping your engineers with React MUI. It offers a wide range of pre-built components like buttons, menus, cards, and more, all styled according to Material Design guidelines. This ensures a consistent and visually appealing UI across your entire web application.

```jsx
import Button from '@mui/material/Button';

function Bridge() {
    return (
        <div>
            <Button variant="contained" color="primary">
                Engage Warp Drive
            </Button>
            <Button variant="outlined" color="secondary">
                Raise Shields
            </Button>
        </div>
    );
}
```

Customization and Theming

Imagine needing to adjust the color scheme of your bridge UI to match a specific alert status (red for red alert!). React MUI allows you to customize the appearance of components using props or create custom themes to achieve a unified look and feel for your web-application.

```javascript
import { createTheme, ThemeProvider } from '@mui/material/styles';

const theme = createTheme({
    palette: {
        primary: { main: 'red' }, // Red buttons for red alert!
    },
});

function Bridge() {
    return (
        <ThemeProvider theme={theme}>
            {/* ... bridge UI components */}
        </ThemeProvider>
    );
}
```

Styled components

Styled Components act like your replicator for UI styles, allowing you to define and apply styles directly within your React components using familiar CSS syntax.

Traditional CSS and Challenges

React traditionally uses CSS to style components. Imagine having separate CSS files or inline styles for each component. This approach can become cumbersome for complex UIs, leading to styles scattered throughout your codebase and potential maintenance issues.

```
1   // Bridge.js
2   import './Bridge.css';
3
4   function Bridge() {
5     return (
6       <div className="bridge">
7         {/* Bridge UI elements */}
8       </div>
9     );
10  }
11
12  // Bridge.css
13  .bridge {
14    background-color: #333;
15    color: #fff;
16    padding: 20px;
17  }
```

Styled Components in Action

Styled Components provide a way to write CSS within your JavaScript components. Imagine using a special component like `styled.div` to define styles directly alongside your component's JSX. This keeps styles localized and tightly coupled to the components they apply to.

```javascript
import styled from 'styled-components';

const StyledBridge = styled.div`
  background-color: #333;
  color: #fff;
  padding: 20px;
`;

function Bridge() {
  return (
    <StyledBridge>
      {/* Bridge UI elements */}
    </div>
  );
}
```

Styling Props and Dynamic Styles

Imagine needing the bridge to switch between red alert mode and normal mode. You can define styles within styled components that receive props and adjust styles accordingly.

```javascript
const StyledBridge = styled.div`
  background-color: ${(props) =>
    (props.alert ? 'red' : '#333')};
  color: #fff;
  padding: 20px;
`;

function Bridge(props) {
  return (
    <StyledBridge alert={props.isRedAlert}>
      {/* Bridge UI elements */}
    </div>
  );
}
```

Testing

Why Testing is Important

Imagine a malfunctioning warp core control panel or a crew roster that displays inaccurate information. Testing helps identify and fix these issues before they cause problems on critical missions.

```javascript
// Bridge component with a potential bug (incorrect button click handler)
function Bridge() {
    const handleClick = () => {
        // Incorrect logic here (e.g., missing function call)
    };

    return (
        <div>
            <button onClick={handleClick}>Engage Warp Drive</button>
        </div>
    );
}
```

Testing with Jest

Jest is a popular testing framework for JavaScript applications. Imagine using Jest to write unit tests that specifically target the `Bridge` component and its functionalities. These tests can verify if the button click handler works correctly and triggers the expected actions.

```js
// Bridge.test.js (Jest test file)
import React from 'react';
import { render, screen } from '@testing-library/react';
import Bridge from './Bridge'; // Import the component to test

test('Bridge component renders correctly', () => {
    render(<Bridge />);
    const button = screen.getByRole('button', { name: /Engage Warp Drive/i }); // Find the button by text content
    expect(button).toBeInTheDocument(); // Assert that the button is present
});

test('Bridge button click handler triggers logic', () => {
    const mockLogic = jest.fn(); // Mock function to simulate the expected logic

    render(<Bridge handleClick={mockLogic} />); // Pass the mock function as a prop
    const button = screen.getByRole('button', { name: /Engage Warp Drive/i });
    button.click();

    expect(mockLogic).toHaveBeenCalledTimes(1); // Assert that the mock function was called
});
```

Testing Different Scenarios

Imagine needing to test the bridge under red alert conditions or the crew roster when handling a large number of crew members. You can write multiple tests to simulate these scenarios and ensure your components behave as expected.

```javascript
test('Bridge button displays red text on red alert', () => {
    render(<Bridge isRedAlert={true} />); // Pass prop to simulate red alert
    const button = screen.getByRole('button', { name: /Engage Warp Drive/i });
    expect(button).toHaveStyle({ color: 'red' }); // Assert button text color
});
```

API Calls

react-query

Imagine your crew relies on critical data from various ship systems, like sensor readings, engine performance metrics, and course coordinates. But constantly fetching this data can be inefficient and lead to performance issues. React Query acts like your ship's efficient data management system, streamlining data fetching and caching for your React components, ensuring smooth operation and a responsive user interface.

Challenges of Manual Data Fetching

Traditionally, React components might fetch data directly using libraries like Axios. Imagine having multiple bridge displays, each fetching sensor data, engine readings, and course information from separate API endpoints. This can lead to repetitive code, unnecessary re-fetches of the same data, and potential performance bottlenecks.

```javascript
// EngineMonitor component (simplified example)
function EngineMonitor() {
    const [engineData, setEngineData] = useState(null);

    useEffect(() => {
        const fetchData = async () => {
            const response = await axios.get('/api/engine-data');
            setEngineData(response.data);
        };
        fetchData();
    }, []);

    return (
        <div>
            {/* Display engine data if available */}
        </div>
    );
}
```

Data Fetching with React Query

React Query provides a declarative and automated way to manage data fetching within React applications. Imagine equipping your engineering crew with React Query. It allows you to define queries that specify how and when to fetch data, and then components can simply declare their data dependencies using hooks provided by React Query.

```js
import { useQuery } from 'react-query';

function EngineMonitor() {
    const { isLoading, error, data } = useQuery('engineData', async () => {
        const response = await axios.get('/api/engine-data');
        return response.data;
    });

    if (isLoading) return <div>Loading engine data...</div>;
    if (error) return <div>Error fetching engine data!</div>;

    return (
        <div>
            {/* Display engine data from 'data' */}
        </div>
    );
}
```

Automatic Caching and Refetching

Imagine the sensor readings display constantly refetching data, even if the values haven't changed. React Query automatically caches fetched data and only refetches it when necessary, based on defined caching strategies.

```js
const { isLoading, error, data, refetch } =
useQuery('sensorReadings', async () => {
    // ... logic to fetch sensor data
}, { cacheTime: 5000 }); // Refetch data every 5 seconds
```

```javascript
import axios from 'axios'; // Import Axios library

const handleClick = async () => {
    try {
        const response = await axios.get('https://api.starfleet.com/messages'); // GET request to retrieve messages
        console.log(response.data); // Access response data (received messages)
    } catch (error) {
        console.error(error); // Handle errors during API call
    }
};

```

Forms

Traditional Form Handling

React traditionally handles forms through controlled components and event listeners. Imagine an engineer manually writing code to handle user input in each form field, track validation errors, and submit form data. This approach can be tedious and error-prone, especially for complex forms.

```jsx
function CoursePlotter() {
    const [course, setCourse] = useState('');
    const [error, setError] = useState(null);

    const handleChange = (event) => {
        setCourse(event.target.value);
        setError(null); // Clear previous error on input change
    };

    const handleSubmit = (event) => {
        event.preventDefault();
        if (!isValidCourse(course)) {
            setError('Invalid course format!');
            return;
        }
        // Submit form data (course)
    };

    return (
        <form onSubmit={handleSubmit}>
            <input type="text" value={course} onChange={handleChange} placeholder="Enter Course (e.g., Alpha Centauri)" />
            {error && <div className="error">{error}</div>}
            <button type="submit">Set Course</button>
        </form>
    );
}
```

React Hook Form

React Hook Form is a popular library that simplifies form handling using React hooks. Imagine equipping your engineers with React Hook Form. It provides hooks to manage form state, handle user input, perform validation, and submit data, all in a concise and reusable way.

```jsx
import { useForm } from 'react-hook-form';

function CoursePlotter() {
    const { register, handleSubmit, formState: { errors } } = useForm(); // Get form hooks

    const onSubmit = (data) => {
        console.log(data); // Access submitted form data (course)
        // Submit form data to the server
    };

    return (
        <form onSubmit={handleSubmit(onSubmit)}>
            <input type="text" {...register('course', { required: true, pattern: /^[A-Za-z\s]+$/ })} placeholder="Enter Course" />
            {errors.course && <div className="error">Invalid course format!</div>}
            <button type="submit">Set Course</button>
        </form>
    );
}
```

Validation Made Easy

Imagine ensuring the entered course adheres to a specific format (e.g., letters and spaces only). React Hook Form allows you to define validation rules for each form field and provides informative error messages to the crew.

```
const { register, handleSubmit, formState: { errors } } = useForm();

...

<input type="text" {...register('course', { required: true, pattern: /^[A-Za-z\s]+$/ })} placeholder="Enter Course" />
```

Benefits of React Hook Form

Practice using React Hook Form to streamline form development in your React application. This improves code readability, reduces boilerplate code, and simplifies form management, ensuring your engineers can focus on building robust and user-friendly control panels for your starship.

State Management with Redux

As chief engineer on a massive starship, you face a data deluge! React and state management libraries (like Redux or Context API) are your lifelines. Redux acts as your central ship's brain, a vast database tracking every detail ensuring systems work in harmony. Need to reroute power? Raise shields? Actions and reducers update the central state, and your React displays reflect the changes in real-time. It's like having a specialized engineering team at your command, overseen by your state management solution. React, paired with robust state management, gives you the control needed for mission success.

Traditional State Management

React traditionally manages state within individual components using hooks like `useState`. Imagine an Employee assigned to managing multiple bridge consoles (components) like engine power, shields, and weapons. Each console would have its own state, leading to potential inconsistencies and difficulty in coordinating actions across the bridge.

Example of State management with Redux in a React application

Imagine we have a spaceship component that displays the current status of the ship's systems:

```js
import React from 'react';
import { useSelector } from 'react-redux';

const Spaceship = () => {
  const { engines, shields, crew } = useSelector(state => state);

  return (
    <div>
      <h1>Starship Enterprise</h1>
      <p>Engines Status: {engines.status}</p>
      <p>Shields Status: {shields.status}</p>
      <p>Crew On Board: {crew.count}</p>
    </div>
  );
};

export default Spaceship;
```

In this example, the **Spaceship component** uses the **useSelector** hook from React Redux to access the current state of the ship's engines, shields, and crew. The state is stored in a central Redux store, which acts as the ship's central computer.

Now, let's imagine that the user needs to raise the ship's shields. We can create a Redux action to update the shields' status:

```js
// actions.js
export const raiseShields = () => ({
  type: 'RAISE_SHIELDS',
});
```

The corresponding Redux reducer would look like this:

```javascript
// reducers.js
const initialState = {
  engines: { status: 'nominal' },
  shields: { status: 'lowered' },
  crew: { count: 200 },
};

const rootReducer = (state = initialState, action) => {
  switch (action.type) {
    case 'RAISE_SHIELDS':
      return {
        ...state,
        shields: { status: 'raised' },
      };
    default:
      return state;
  }
};

export default rootReducer;
```

Redux Toolkit

Redux Toolkit acts like your ship's central command center, providing a simplified and organized approach to state management within your React application.

Traditional Redux

Redux is a popular state management library for JavaScript applications. However, setting up Redux can involve boilerplate code and require writing separate logic for reducers, actions, and selectors. To resolve this issue, we use the Redux Toolkit add-on library.

```javascript
// Redux reducer (simplified example)
const initialState = { enginePower: 50, shieldStrength: 70 };

function rootReducer(state = initialState, action) {
  switch (action.type) {
    case 'INCREASE_ENGINE_POWER':
      return { ...state, enginePower: state.enginePower + 10 };
    case 'DECREASE_ENGINE_POWER':
      return { ...state, enginePower: state.enginePower - 10 };
    // ...reducers for other actions
    default:
      return state;
  }
}

// Bridge component (simplified example)
function Bridge() {
  const dispatch = useDispatch();

  const increaseEnginePower = () => dispatch({ type: 'INCREASE_ENGINE_POWER' });
  const decreaseEnginePower = () => dispatch({ type: 'DECREASE_ENGINE_POWER' });

  return (
    <div>
      <button onClick={increaseEnginePower}>Increase Engine Power</button>
      <button onClick={decreaseEnginePower}>Decrease Engine Power</button>
      {/* Display engine power based on state */}
    </div>
  );
}
```

Redux Toolkit

Redux Toolkit is an official add-on library for Redux that simplifies common tasks and streamlines state management. It provides functions like `createSlice` to define reducers, actions, and selectors in a more concise and readable way, reducing boilerplate code and improving maintainability.

```javascript
import { createSlice } from '@reduxjs/toolkit';

const initialState = { enginePower: 50, shieldStrength: 70 };

const bridgeSlice = createSlice({
  name: 'bridge',
  initialState,
  reducers: {
    increaseEnginePower: (state) => {
      state.enginePower += 10;
    },
    decreaseEnginePower: (state) => {
      state.enginePower -= 10;
    },
  },
});

export const { increaseEnginePower, decreaseEnginePower } = bridgeSlice.actions;
export default bridgeSlice.reducer;

// Bridge component using Redux Toolkit (simplified example)
function Bridge() {
  const dispatch = useDispatch();
  const state = useSelector((state) => state.bridge); // Access state using useSelector

  return (
    <div>
      <button onClick={() => dispatch(increaseEnginePower())}>Increase Engine Power</button>
      <button onClick={() => dispatch(decreaseEnginePower())}>Decrease Engine Power</button>
      {/* Display engine power based on state.enginePower */}
    </div>
  );
}
```

Immutable Updates and Async Operations

Imagine needing to update shield strength based on incoming enemy fire (which might be asynchronous). Redux Toolkit enforces immutable state updates and provides utilities for handling asynchronous actions and side effects within reducers.

Benefits of Redux Toolkit

It simplifies Redux setup, reduces boilerplate code, and improves the organization and maintainability of your application's state. It ensures a clear separation of concerns between components and state management logic.

About the Author

Rishi Gujadhur is an experienced full-stack engineer with over 4 years of expertise in software development. His technical skills include proficiency in .NET, .NET Core, React, Redux, DevOps practices using Azure and GitHub, and microservices architecture using MassTransit and Kafka. Rishi has held positions at Ceridian Mauritius and SD Worx Mauritius, contributing to software development and maintenance. He also has internship experience at SBM Bank Mauritius and Ceridian, working on projects like chatbot development, mapping applications, and knowledge base software. Rishi's background demonstrates a well-rounded skill set, a passion for software development, and a strong track record of success.